# THE CHURCH'S MINISTRY
## IN OUR TIME

# School of Divinity

Gardner-Webb University
School of Divinity

# THE
# CHURCH'S MINISTRY
# IN OUR TIME

*By*

HENRY KNOX SHERRILL

NEW YORK
CHARLES SCRIBNER'S SONS
1949

To
B. H. S.

## FOREWORD

THE FIRST two chapters in this book, I believe, are realistic rather than pessimistic. It is my conviction that the Christian must face courageously the stern facts of contemporary life both without and within the Church. Only by so doing can we be saved from the strange (in the light of present conditions) complacency which so easily besets us to such a great extent that many of us with good intentions are content to be at ease in Zion. The remaining chapters emphasize the overwhelming spiritual resources which God has given to us. Our world can be redeemed through an inspired and sacrificial Church. But there can only be such a Church as there are men and women of deep conviction who have responded to the call of God in Christ.

This book comprises the Lyman Beecher Lectures delivered last April. I am deeply grateful to President Seymour, Dean Weigle and the faculty of the Yale Divinity School for the opportunity of giving these lectures. I shall always remember the stimulation

and the friendliness of the hours spent in the fellowship of the faculty, students and alumni of the
School.

Although he must not be held responsible for any
of the opinions expressed in these pages, I am greatly
indebted to my former teacher at the Episcopal
Theological School, the Very Reverend H. E. W.
Fosbroke, D. D., Dean Emeritus of the General Theological Seminary in New York City, for encouragement and helpful suggestion, so characteristic of his
generous friendship of almost forty years.

HENRY KNOX SHERRILL

December 1948

# CONTENTS

# THE CHURCH'S MINISTRY
## IN OUR TIME

# I

## THE SPIRITUAL STATE
## OF THE WORLD

"AND THERE shall be signs in the sun and in the moon and in the stars; and upon the earth distress of nations with perplexity; the sea and the waves roaring; men's hearts failing them for fear, and for looking after those things which are coming on the earth: for the powers of heaven shall be shaken."

These are words which are often taken as figurative. Whether that interpretation be true or not they are a realistic description of our times. "Men's hearts are failing them for fear and for looking after those things which are coming on the earth." We live in an apocalyptic day which may well prove to be a turning point in history. What is the meaning of the signs of the times? Are we witnessing the death throes of a civilization or are these portents the birth pangs of a new and nobler society which is to be? The answer is not easy to reach. We are necessarily children of our own generation. As a result it is well nigh impossible to judge objectively. We cannot see the woods for the trees. One can read of the rise and fall of Greece and of Rome with complete objectivity. We can assess the spiritual value attained by the world in the destruction of Jerusalem in the sixth century B.C. and the captivity of so many thousands. But how different to have been one of the company who sat down by the waters of Babylon and wept! How few there were who had any understanding of the message and the significance of Jesus of Nazareth or of St. Paul in their generation. In modern times the misinterpretation of both Washington and Lincoln, while they lived, is astounding to those of a later day. To view the events of today with wisdom is extremely difficult because we lack perspective and are bound to see them somewhat out of focus. We are not spectators of a drama enacted upon a stage. We are in the cast ourselves. We, and our children, our security, our hopes, yes— and our fears, are deeply involved.

Within recent years attempts have been made to evaluate civilizations. Oswald Spengler in his *Decline of the West* has tried to draw an analogy between the failure and death of civilizations and the physical decay of the human body. He argues that cultures grow old and die as do men, that the course of the life span can be estimated by diagnosis and that the future, or at least the lack of future, is more or less predictable. More recently Arnold Toynbee has engaged from a different angle in a study of civilizations, living and dead. Toynbee quotes Spengler: "A civilization is born when out of the primitive psychic conditions of a perpetually infantile (raw) humanity, a mighty soul awakes and extricates itself; a form out of the formless, a bounded and transitory existence out of the boundless and persistent. This soul comes to flower on the soil of a country with precise boundaries, to which it remains attached like a plant. Conversely a civilization dies if once this soul has realized the complete sum of its possibilities in the shape of peoples, languages, creeds, arts, states and sciences and thereupon goes back into the primitive psyche from which it originally emerged.[1] Here is a philosophy of utter and complete pessimism. It reminds me of a popular song of Raymond Hitchcock's, entitled, *What's The Use?*, and I recall the line, "What's the use of people growing old and dying if they must be born again?" It is the ancient pagan theory of purposeless cycles. Toynbee goes on to say: "The biological and psychological analogies are manifestly unsuited to express the relation in which growing civilizations stand to their individual members."[2] He writes with

[1] Arnold Toynbee (Abridged by D. C. Somervell), *A Study of History*, pp. 210-211, Copyright 1946 by Oxford University Press, N. Y., Inc.

[2] *Ibid.*, p. 254.

3

Christian faith and hope: "This is a message of encouragement for us children of the Western civilization as we drift today alone with none but stricken civilizations around us. It may be that Death the Leveller will lay his icy hand on our civilization also. But we are not comforted with any *Saeva Necessitas*. The dead civilizations are not dead by fate or in the course of nature and therefore our living civilization is not doomed inexorably in advance to join the majority of its species. Though sixteen civilizations may have perished to our knowledge and nine others may be now at the point of death, we, the twenty-sixth are not compelled to submit the riddle of our fate to the blind arbitrament of statistics. The divine spark of creative power is still alive in us and if we have grace to kindle it into flame, then the stars in their courses cannot defeat our efforts to attain the goal of human endeavor." [3] There we have a complete contrast to Spengler. But somehow the analyses of the dead past in both of these studies seems more certain than that of the living present. Perhaps because we know so much more of today with opinions and prejudices of our own, the illustrations from ancient times seem more conclusive than those drawn from modern America and Europe. The pathologist

[3] *Ibid.*, p. 254.

4

can be more accurate in his verdict as to the cause of death than can the physician in his diagnosis of the state of health of the living patient. However, admitting the difficulty, it is essential that we attempt to have some understanding of where we are and, more important, in what direction we are moving. If we are fatalists, then all we can hope to do is to drift with what resignation we can muster with the tide. But if we are Christian, then our faith tells us that we can do all things through Christ who strengthens us. The Christian by that very fact cannot be a defeatist or a coward. But to act wisely we must know to some degree where we stand. The Master ridiculed those who could read the heavens but who could not discern the signs of the times.

Of one fact we may be very clear. To quote Dr. Elton Trueblood, our civilization is sick. Gone is the easy-going optimism so prevalent before 1914 when human progress, prosperity and peace were regarded as inevitable as the rise of the tide and to make confession of sin was an affront to the intelligence and to the dignity of man.

Even the most thoughtless cannot escape the fact of two devastating world wars. In 1914 it at first seemed incredible that men could be actually fighting and dying by the thousands. The Civil War was history. The Boer and the Russo-Japanese Wars in those days were far removed from our American orbit. The episode in Cuba had been a comic opera affair. But in 1914 our house of cards fell. Then in 1918 and 1919 came the great and exaggerated hope of peace. We had won the war and now we were assuredly to achieve Mr. Wilson's goal to "Make the world safe for democracy." Succeeding events are too recent to need recounting. There followed the unreal prosperity of the twenties, the great depression, the rise of Mussolini and Hitler in the uneasy thirties, until again war broke upon us, leaving a world in which destruction, want, suspicion and hatred are rampant. Even today, unless one has seen with one's own eyes, it is difficult to realize the conditions in which millions of our fellows are attempting to live. The present plight of thousands upon thousands of so-called displaced persons is a blot upon our civilization. No written word, no picture still or moving, can portray the terrible actuality of complete destruction with attendant privation and suffering. Now again we have won a military victory, this time with only a cautious, somewhat cynical hope of peace. Still the same problems of cooperation and of understanding between men and nations are before us. We pass from one international conference to the next, from one crisis to another. Yet all the time we know, not from the preachers, but from the scientists the inevitable price of another war. One gets a picture of little men struggling with events and with forces too great for them to control, even to face. Germany and Japan are prostrate. Hitler and Mussolini have passed from the stage of current history but still the problems remain, the sickness is unabated. This is one of the indications that wars are but symptoms of an even deeper disease. History cannot be too greatly simplified, as Professor Sidney B. Fay's study of the origins of the first world war has shown. The skein is too tangled and reaches far back into the past. There is the burden of sin not only of ourselves but of preceding generations. The whole human family to a greater or less degree is involved in the causes of war. Caught in the web of their own weaving men already talk and prepare for the next war. What is the cause of this sickness? Some will say economic rivalry, others the selfish desire for power, others ideological differences. Certainly extreme nationalism is one strong reason. All of these factors and many more must be dealt with realistically and overcome. The United Nations is of course an essential step in this direction but no schemes of organization, no matter how hopeful, will solve the problem and cure our ills. The true cause rests in the minds and hearts of men. As Professor Toynbee has written, "In demonstrating that the broken down

7

civilizations have not met their death from an assassin's hand, we have found no reason to dispute the allegation that they have been victims of violence and in almost every instance we have been led by the logical process of exhaustion to return a verdict of suicide. In tragic life, God wot, no villain need be! Passions spin the plot. We are betrayed by what is false within." [4]

Dr. Trueblood is correct when he writes, "It is important to make it abundantly clear at this point that the crucial problem is the spiritual problem and we here mean by spiritual that area which is the object of attention in philosophy and theology as against that area in which the object of attention is mechanical contrivance." [5] The hard facts have dealt a death blow to our belief in inevitable progress. Similarly in the light of these same facts it is difficult to hold faith in the goodness of man by himself. But the breakdown of these two articles of nineteenth- and twentieth-century faith has in the meantime caused men to lose touch with what may be called in the largest terms the objective life of the Spirit. Before the war Professor Etienne Gilson in a lecture at the Harvard Tercentenary predicted the inevitable disunity because men had forgotten the only source

[4] *Ibid.*, p. 275.

[5] Elton Trueblood, *Predicament of Modern Man*, p. 16, Harpers.

of unity in God. This is true not of one but of all religions, nations and people. It is a world phenomenon.

The case of Germany, of course, gives us the most striking example—for here we see the common faults of men carried to the extreme—if it were not so tragic, to the *reductio ad absurdum*. We have at home our extreme nationalist isolationists, our upholders of white supremacy, our worshippers of the supreme state. In Germany all this was carried to a logical and terrible conclusion. Here was a country for many centuries at least outwardly Christian—the nation of many saints, heroes, philosophers and scholars, Roman Catholic and Protestant. Suddenly, almost without warning, the nation tolerates the most cruel persecution and engages in a war as an aggressor nation under a fantastic leadership, armed with a so-called philosophy which was worse than a reversion to respectable paganism. A prominent anti-Nazi once told me that a million fanatical Nazis had eighty million Germans by the throat. But that explanation even if true can hardly explain how such a *tour de force* could be possible. Granted strict military discipline and censorship, the German people must have known what was going on. There must have been a tremendous weakening of the spiritual faith and the moral stamina of the great

majority of Germans who were at best nominally
Christian. In December, 1945, it was my duty to
visit Germany as one of a delegation representing
the Federal Council of Churches in order to confer
with the leaders of the German Churches. In many
ways it was a deeply moving experience. Many of
these German Churchmen had proved their loyalty
to Christ by spending months to years in concentration camps. Many of them were men of the truest
Christian spirit. I recall one pastor, whose life had
been saved only by the speedy arrival of our troops,
exclaiming with tears in his eyes, "I am guilty that
I am alive in the light of what my nation has done."
Poorly clad and underfed, meeting in rooms so cold
that many times we all wore our overcoats, they reminded their visitors of the atmosphere and the temper of mind of the early Church. These men are a
glory to the Christian Church and Faith. Professor
Einstein's tribute to them is well deserved. They remained constant to the last when many others in the
ranks of labor, of the universities and elsewhere, had
fallen away. I believe with all my heart that in this
minority of clergy and people is to be found the hope
of Germany and that those who have passed through
this ordeal-by-fire unscathed in spirit if not in body
have much to give to us of other nations and
Churches. But that does not change the hard fact

that they were a very small minority, and that the German people did allow such events to happen in their midst with their tacit, if not with their always open, consent. I write this with no feeling of superiority but simply that we may be able to face the situation before us. Here is a fact—with all honor to the faithful few, Protestant and Roman Catholic, who remained true to their Master, something was terribly lacking in the understanding and the practice of the Christianity of the great majority of the German people and nation. Granted that they were misinformed, shut off from world opinion, nevertheless that cannot be a complete explanation. We must have it one, not both, ways. We can thank God for evidences of great personal faith and courage but we cannot and must not forget the lesson of the collapse of a nation which for many centuries had been called Christian. If this can happen in one nation, it can happen in others.

Just before the end of the war, I visited Great Britain. There has been a great deal of ill-informed talk that the war with its resulting suffering and hardship developed the spiritual life. This sort of impression seems always to be evident in time of war. As was seen to be true in the case of Germany, numerous individuals did reveal great spiritual power, but as in Germany this was not correct as regards the great majority of people in Great Britain.

As we all know there was evidence of dogged determination but there was also a spiritual apathy. The terrible events of the present, combined with other factors, had proved too great a load for faith as any kind of buoyant conviction and expression. Rather, men and women held on because there was nothing else to do. The difficult post-war years I fear will only increase this tendency. Certainly there were no indications of anything which could remotely be described as a religious revival.

The report of the Archbishop's Commission on Evangelism entitled *Towards the Conversion of England* bears out completely this necessarily surface impression. "There can be no doubt," the report states, "that there is a widespread gulf between the Church and the people. The evidence of Chaplains and others in close touch with all these services and with munition factories may be accepted as conclusive. They testify with one voice to the fact of a wholesale drift from organized religion. The present irrelevance of the Church in the life and thought of the community in general is apparent from two symptoms which admit of no dispute. They are one, the widespread decline in Church-going, and two, the collapse of Christian moral standards. It is indisputable that only a small percentage of the nation today joins in public worship of any kind." [6] A footnote adds, "It has recently been estimated that from 10% to 15% of the population are closely linked to some Christian Church; that 25% to 30% are sufficiently interested to attend a place of worship upon great occasions; that 45% to 50% are indifferent to religion though more or less friendly-disposed towards it; while 10% to 20% are hostile. It is open to question which is the more alarming feature, the failure of the Church to attract or its failure to repel." The report goes on to discuss the collapse of Christian moral standards. "If we have seemed to emphasize the declension from Christian moral standards more particularly in the realm of sex it is because it is most obtrusive in this field, not because it is not marked in other directions. The sense of duty and of responsibility has become undermined. There is no longer an accepted moral standard by which men judge their own standard. The idea of man as a responsible person is in danger of disappearing with the loss of belief in the living God. No wonder our generation has been dubbed the age without standards." [7] I have quoted at length from this report because in it we have the considered judgment of a competent and official commission of the Church of England. There

[6] Pp. 2-3, Press and Publications Board of the Church Assembly, London, Republished by J. M. Dent & Sons, Ltd. (Canada).

[7] *Ibid.*, p. 5.

will be those who will take comfort in the admitted fact that religion is broader than the organized Churches and that failure to attend Church may not always be the measure of the spiritual life of a nation. But on the other hand we may well recall a sentence of Baron von Hugel—that we no longer say a man stays away from Church through the sheer fervor of his personal religion. The fact is that religious conditions in Great Britain are a matter of great concern to those who know and care the most.

The great Roman Catholic countries of Europe, and of Central and South America, are of less immediate importance to us because the entire picture is so markedly different from ours. But it is true that in France and Italy, our chaplains, many of them Roman Catholic, expressed even stronger opinions than those contained in the Church of England report. It is evident that the collapse of France and Italy was caused by much more than military weakness. Today in Russia there are undoubtedly many millions of spiritually-minded men and women. The experience of God in Christ cannot be uprooted in a brief span of years. Bishop Tucker likes to tell of the fact that many years before Commodore Perry visited Japan, Roman Catholic missionaries had gone there. They and their converts suffered a cruel and apparently decisive persecution. Yet when Christian missionaries returned after many decades, they found that certain Christian teachings and rites had lived underground and been passed on from one generation to another. But while all that may be confidently hoped for in connection with the Russian people, the fact is that a government has come into power which, to put the case mildly and uncontroversially, can in no way be described as even nominally Christian.[8] Whatever one may have thought of the state of official religion under the czars, the present régime does not promise much from the point of view of the Christian religion.

The trend in the West is also marked in the East. One of the great opportunities for the spread of the Gospel in the Orient has long been recognized as the result of the breakdown of ancient religions due to the undermining impact of Western civilization. The picture sometimes drawn by those who belittle Christian missions, of a happy Near East and East devoted to their own religion, is a figment of the imagination. The truth is that leaving aside for the present our own country and South America, which has long presented problems of deep religious faith, wide-

[8] Last summer I spent several hours with a clergyman of the Russian church. He stated that there is freedom of religious worship in Russia with the exception that no person under eighteen could be taught religion by the Church except by means of the sermon. This statement I believe to be true but it is worship without any relation to the determining factors of economics or politics. It is worship removed from application to society.

spread skepticism, with low educational and moral standards, so far as great masses of the population are concerned, throughout the world there has been a great weakening in what may be called in the most general terms the life of the spirit.

Here at home the facts are not dissimilar. There are those who find great encouragement in the statistics of church membership, but the significance of these figures demands close examination before they can be taken as meaning a deep experience of the Christian Faith. There is always a danger that we glorify the past unjustifiably. A book of Henry Drummond's written in the middle of the nineteenth century is almost a complete replica of the recent Church of England report to which reference has been made. We tend to exaggerate the virtues of a simpler America. The so-called "good old days" probably never existed. Nevertheless it is incontrovertible that we have lost moral poise and balance—not to mention deep spiritual conviction. No doubt much of this is due to changed conditions. The urbanization and the mechanization of life have exacted a heavy toll—with a strain particularly upon the home and the family. As a result there are tremendous moral problems to be faced and to be solved.

The increase in the divorce rate is a well known and alarming fact. Once this seemed to be a matter of statistics but now the truth permeates every group in society. It is a situation with which we are all personally acquainted in the tragedies of personal friends. An editorial in the *Boston Herald* has the suggestive heading, "Decline of Monogamy." This article goes on to state that in 1887 there was one divorce in America for every seventeen marriages, while in 1945, according to the Metropolitan Life Insurance Company, there was one divorce for every three and two-tenths marriages. The Hollywood situation would be regarded as a parody were it not a dramatization of what is happening in and to our society.

There are many reasons for this, certainly one of them is a loose standard of sexual morality. I have before me a Bulletin of the American Social Hygiene Association which states: "Venereal disease is spreading. Except for the common cold and measles, venereal disease strikes more people each year than any other communicable disease known to the United States." The folder then continues very properly in the interest of health, "Alarming as the situation is America has all the instruments at hand for victory over venereal disease in the foreseeable future—science knows the cause, science knows the cure. The way to control lies in application of the instruments we have at hand. And the most important of these is education—popular and professional." Here is a great campaign to be waged for health. This demands the removal of false ideas of prudery. The American people must know and face the facts and of course we must use all the weapons of modern medical science especially to prevent the suffering of the innocent. But science, however powerful and successful in preventing and curing the disease, cannot control the field of human weakness and desire. Many were shocked by the revelation of sexual promiscuity in the armed forces during the war. There were of course special reasons, due to long absence from home, the abnormal circumstances of life, which made these conditions what they were. But we should have no illusions. The situation in military life is not greatly different from that existing under ordinary conditions. In the armed forces the facts were known. A soldier and a sailor have no personal privacy. In civilian life their affairs are in large measure secret. Many a young chaplain leaving his home Church circle found himself thrown into an alien and staggering environment. Yet that environment was there at home, only a veneer of civilization concealed the fact. Let us make no mistake, we face more than a battle to prevent and control venereal disease. The struggle is to instill the simplest standards of morality and of self-discipline.

The breakdown of family life has created in large measure the problem of youth. Children lacking home training and atmosphere roam the streets of our cities so that juvenile delinquency has become a major concern of government. Our courts and our reformatories are crowded with offenders who are in many cases little more than children. The tragedy of broken homes exacts a toll on more than one generation.

In general the moral climate is low. Let us take for example our literature. It makes no difference the portion of society described, the result is similar whether we take the novels of John Steinbeck, or the satires of Sinclair Lewis, or the accurate reporting of John Marquand. In Steinbeck we have a picture of understandable vulgarity due as in *Grapes of Wrath* to impossible conditions of life. In Lewis and Marquand, with more sophisticated and wealthier characters, there is an almost complete absence of any quality which might be remotely described as spiritual. These books make an appeal because they have the touch of reality. They are photographic. All of us know people with the same outlook, the identical habits and philosophy. Again and again I have read reviews in high praise of modern fiction, only to find in the books themselves a moral and spiritual vacuum. It was the same atmosphere which was found in army barracks and may be found in the rest rooms of factories, in smoking cars on the trains, or in country clubs.

Grossness either in high places or low, while the most obvious, is not the most disturbing factor in our contemporary scene. The Master understood and forgave the woman taken in adultery but found it infinitely more difficult to deal with those animated by pride and by concern for outward respectability. We talk much of our American way of life but we should be blind were we to ignore evidences of bitter intolerance and of cruel discrimination. This is true of every section of the country. In New England, where I have lived for many years, the condition exists as any one who takes the trouble may observe. I have a Negro friend who for eighteen years drove my car as I went about Massachusetts. Again and again I was shocked by the humiliations which he was forced to undergo.

There is much in our American way we can admire, but there is also here a certain ruthlessness, a struggle for power, an emphasis upon the control and the possession of things which is far removed from the Christian way. It is a curious fact that war which stresses the same factors so often acts as a moral tonic. Perhaps it is the realization of a common danger and the necessity of a common effort. It is notable in war time how the entire population accepts restrictions, is willing to make sacrifices, and how all groups work together for a common objective. Then when the pressure of fear is removed, there is not sufficient compulsion in love. In war time we reduce speed to conserve tires, but in peace we cannot do this to save human lives. In war there is to an impressive extent cooperation between labor and capital. Almost the moment the military war ends, we witness an outbreak of the industrial struggle. Countless illustrations of this strange fact of the moral let-down in time of peace come to mind. Here too are unlovely, even dangerous, factors to be understood and to be faced.

We come back to Dr. Trueblood's statement that the crucial problem is the spiritual problem. We have seen how there has been everywhere a deterioration of the life of the spirit. We in this country have placed the greatest reliance upon education. It has been an effort only described adequately as mass production. Certainly in our schools and universities we should hope to find clear leadership in this matter. But the fact is that education as much as any other field has been influenced by the trend of the times. No one of us has the right to be overcritical or self-righteous because in greater or less degree, this is true of ourselves. We are all of us necessarily children of our own day and generation. Because of the separation of Church and State, public institutions have never been able to do much with religious education. Because there are Catholics, Protestants and Jews, the net result is no religious practice and instruction. Under existing conditions this may be necessary but let us clearly understand that we pay a tremendous price as a result. With diminished and in many cases no religious instruction in the home and with none in the schools, is it any wonder that our youth is ignorant of religion?

Our greatest private universities and colleges were founded especially to meet this condition—to train men and women to be Christian citizens in a democracy with the emphasis upon Christian. Still in these institutions there may be found the outward observance of this fact in chapels and chaplains, in services, sermons, and public prayers. In every school and college there is a minority still true to the spiritual ideal of the founders but it is a minority. Along with much else in our civilization these become secularized—despite the well-known and readily admitted fact that on these faculties may be found countless men and women who are humanitarians and idealists, giving of themselves with great unselfishness to the common good. A perfect illustration is found in the report of the Harvard Committee entitled, *General*

*Education in a Free Society.*[9] This report is in no sense peculiar to Harvard but is characteristic of education in general. The same ideas could well have been expressed by similar committees elsewhere.

The report states several times that "A supreme need of American education is for a unifying purpose and idea." But this in the judgment of the writers is not to be achieved by religion, for they state, "This then or something like this is the present state; an enormous variety of aim and method among colleges as a whole and much the same variety on a smaller scale within any one college. This condition which seemingly robs liberal education of any clear coherent meaning has for some time disturbed people and prompted a variety of solutions. Sectarian, particularly Roman Catholic, colleges have, of course, their solution which was generally shared by American colleges until less than a century ago; namely the conviction that Christianity gives meaning and ultimate unity to all parts of the curriculum, indeed to the whole life of the college. Yet this solution is out of the question in publicly supported colleges and is practically, if not legally, impossible in most others. Some think it the Achilles heel of democracy that by its very nature it cannot foster general agreement on ultimates, and perhaps must foster the contrary. But

[9] P. 39, Harvard University Press.

23

whatever one's views, religion is not now for most colleges a practicable source of intellectual unity." I have quoted at length from this report, because the language is so definite. Yet through it all there is a pathetic yearning for ultimates, for something worthwhile which now seems to be lost. At the moment we are not interested in discussing educational theory and objective. The point is that education reveals the same sickness which afflicts the whole of our civilization. As in political life no amount of talk about democracy can change this fact, so no amount of educational phraseology in this area can blind us to the present situation. Our civilization is desperately ill, because we have lost hold upon God.

All of this seems discouraging and pessimistic but, as I have stated, it is imperative that we try to understand clearly in what direction we are moving. The picture is by no means hopeless. Never before have so many millions of men and women everywhere longed so poignantly for peace, for a better way and a better life. When Mr. Wendell Willkie went around the world, he wrote of the great "reservoirs of goodwill" he found for the United States. Whether these remain so for the United States in the post-war world is not so important as that amid hatred and misunderstanding there do exist in every country great reservoirs of goodwill. Here at home there is much of intolerance, bestiality and cruelty, but here again it is true that there have never before been such clear facing of the facts and organized effort toward the elimination of these evils. Though progress seems indeed slow, nevertheless there is progress. The war revealed many weaknesses in American life, yet it also showed much heroic self-sacrifice. A young soldier wrote me from camp of the constant obscenity and immorality. When I replied that one must learn to be in and not of the world, he wrote, "I am sorry that you took what I wrote seriously. It is all true but on the other hand I have never been with such an unselfish group. They would give their right arm for one another." In battle and out of battle these characteristics were revealed. With all the crudity of contemporary American life, there are nevertheless a great generosity and a desire to serve. Vast sums are given for worthy causes and once the heart is touched, a ready response is assured. Our troops abroad fought with no desire for national gain and power, or for personal reward. All they wished to do was to get the task over as quickly as possible and to return to home and to civilian life. What was true of American manhood is true of human nature. We have witnessed terrible degradation of humanity in our generation but in every nation there have been many evidences of high idealism and of heroic self-sacrifice.

In times of discouragement we can well recall the words of the Psalmist: "Yea, and I had almost said even as they; but lo, then I should have condemned the generation of thy children." There is in the hearts of men that "light which lighteth every man which cometh into the world." It is possible to find in men the working of God's Holy Spirit. The Christian desires to face reality however discouraging this may be, but he never does so with despair.

This I believe to be true, but we dare not rest back upon the easy assumption that as a result we need have no responsibility. Abroad danger comes from the paralyzing effect of discouragement and apparent hopelessness. Here at home despite all the evidence before us the danger comes from complacency. To travel from Europe to the United States by plane is within a few hours to pass from one extreme to the other. The difference has to be experienced to be understood. Even yet we have not had it burned into our minds and hearts—that our times need to be redeemed. We speak too lightly of sin and of suffering. The iron has not truly entered into our souls. It is this fact which should cause the deepest concern. The first requisite for health is to realize, if it is present, that sickness exists. That sickness of our civilization, of our society, seems to be proved beyond any doubt. The cause lies not in things, or in nature. The moment the war ended, and men put aside their arms to plant, the earth was ready to bring forth seed time and harvest. The cause must be found in the hearts and the minds of men. It is not enough to clear away rubble and to rebuild cities, bridges and railroads. It is not enough even to devise organizations and new methods to keep and enforce the peace. It is not enough to maintain and extend democracy as a political force. Edith Cavell said prophetically, "Patriotism is not enough." The spiritual walls of Jerusalem are laid waste. It is these which must be rebuilt.

# II

## THE SPIRITUAL STATE OF THE CHURCHES

WE HAVE concluded a rapid survey of the spiritual condition of our civilization. What can we say of the Christian Church in these times? The evidence is in many ways confusing. There are very definite grounds for encouragement. On the other hand as in the case of our general culture, we must beware of contenting ourselves with an easy-going complacency under the guise of Christian faith and hope. There are deep reasons for belief in God's ultimate victory but this should not be confused with the failure to face the realities of our own inadequacy and blindness.

The Twentieth Century Fund recently published a survey of economic conditions in the United States.[1] In this book is a chapter on "Religion and Private Welfare." Let it be said that no statistics can be regarded as infallible especially when dealing with the life of the Spirit. Nevertheless here is an impar-

[1] J. Frederic Dewhurst, *America's Needs and Resources*, p .326.

tial survey which at least must make us consider not only the present strength of the Christian Churches but also the direction in which we are moving. The opening paragraph sums up the general result of this study:

"Organized religion and private social welfare represent a relatively small and apparently declining share of our economic life. It appears that consumers have devoted to the support of the churches and welfare institutions little more than $1.50 out of every $100 of their expenditures in recent years. This is considerably less than we spend for either tobacco or alcoholic beverages. Moreover the share of consumption expenditures going to religious and welfare institutions has been declining." [2]

The report goes on to discuss the salaries of clergymen—(the average throughout the nation for resident clergymen was in 1936 $1,158 as compared with $1,530 in 1924) the inadequate training of the clergy, Church membership, Church attendance and Sunday school enrollment and other topics of less significance. The general conclusions are not encouraging. The Church at the best, and we all know the unreality of Church lists, can claim not more than one half of the total population of the nation. The survey in regard to Church attendance declares:

[2] *Ibid.*

"Only the Congregational Christian Churches have systematically studied Church attendance over a period of years. Their Commission on Church attendance says in its 1934 report that the figures indicate that 70% of the seats in churches are not being used on Sunday mornings, and probably 75% of persons known as members are not supporting their Churches with their personal attendance and active encouragement." [3] Singularly enough and contrary to popular impression the forty-three large Protestant denominations had a combined rate of growth almost identical with that of the Roman Catholic Church. Sunday school enrollment has been steadily decreasing since the turn of the century. Here is the general tenor of the report. We must not get these figures out of focus. Statistics cannot tell the story of faith or of prayer or of spiritual victory. Perhaps the Churches will be stronger spiritually as they become weaker numerically and materially. All I say is that here are evidences which should blast our complacency and should drive us to the most consecrated thought and action.

The most patent fact about the Church which claims to be the Body of Christ is that it is sorely divided. Even in the face of the overwhelming truth that ours is a pagan society and that Christian forces

[3] *Ibid.*

face an unrelenting and desperate battle, this still continues to be true. According to the Twentieth Century Fund survey there are 250 denominations. Later on I shall refer to the growing cooperation in the Ecumenical Movement. However encouraging and hopeful that may be the fact remains that the Body of Christ is divided into many fragments. It is not necessary to enumerate the divisions and subdivisions. The evidence is known to us all in every city, in many towns and even in hamlets. The so-called Church pages published on Saturday mornings in the metropolitan press offer the would-be worshipper a wide but a bewildering choice of preachers, sermon topics and musical offerings.

We have had pointed out to us the economic waste of such a procedure—the cost of many Church buildings, staffs, organists, sextons, heat, light, clerical salaries. In the majority of cases there are small congregations in comparison with the available seating capacity. Beyond question all of this is true from the point of view of efficiency and finance but is, I believe, practically beside the main point because it does not take into account convictions and also an extraordinary depth of sentiment. Even in the same communion where there are no differences of faith or of order it is extremely difficult to unite parishes. I know because I have tried. There is great devotion to the Church building, to the memorials, to the associations of the years. The Church has shown an amazing tenacity through two thousand years of changing world order. Something of that spirit pertains to almost every small fragment of the Church. I recall one section of a city with three churches of one faith. Due to a changing population, one parish could easily have taken care of the spiritual needs of the people. The three rectors agreed to resign, but it was impossible to accomplish the result desired because of the sentimental attachment to the locations and the buildings with all the associations of many years. Still the three congregations held on for many years. All of which tends to prove that we shall not solve the problem of Church unity by the surveys of efficiency experts and this is perhaps as it should be.

A much more serious matter than that of unwise management is that the divided Church makes impossible a united attack upon the forces of paganism and of indifference. The foreign missionary field gives the clearest illustration of this. The differences between the Churches have come about through complex causes over many years, as witness, for example, the divisions caused by the Civil War in this country. All of these divisions are now perpetuated in a country like China. As some one has said: "It is not sensible to ask a Chinaman in North China to belong to the Southern Baptist Church." The confusions and the misunderstandings are evident to the point of absurdity. The serious result is to limit our power to present the central truths of Christianity to win men and women to the knowledge and love of God as revealed in Christ. What is true abroad is equally so at home. The divided Church makes extremely difficult the approach to the pagan and the indifferent in our own society. Furthermore these differences, significant and important as they are, lead us to lose sight of the primary purpose which is again to win men to God. We spend countless time in discussing the peripheries of Christian faith and order.

Canon F. R. Barry of Westminster Abbey (now Bishop of Southwell) has written in his book, *The Relevance of the Church:* "The stream of history has flowed far since the days when the Churches became divided. It is now scarcely possible to maintain that the lines of denominational demarcation correspond with spiritual reality. True that each of the separated Churches came into being in order to witness to some one aspect of the truth. True, as we have already emphasized, that each of these various traditions has its place of right in the Universal Church and must not be overwhelmed in a standardized Christianity. But much that was in the past distinctive has now become part of the common legacy. Divisions that were at the time inspired by positive and constructive convictions are now becoming negative and unreal."[4]

The Church loses constantly in the approach to secular authority because there are so many and so varied groups, convictions and voices. The result is that administrators and legislators are inclined to pay scant heed. Any clergyman who has been a chaplain in the armed forces can testify as to the reality of this fact out of the experience of his own loneliness and at times futility. It is true that indifference only gives way to strength and almost never to weakness. The forces of evil are powerful beyond words to portray. We of our generation have had convincing proof of this fact. We can never bring to bear the power of Christ until we can act as the Body of Christ. The lessons of two world wars have proved beyond question to military leaders the necessity of united nations, of a unified military command to overcome the opposing enemy. This is equally valid for the Church. If we think that we can win the world to Christ by divided councils and witness, a rude awakening is not far off in this day of rapidly moving events. The lessons of peace are clear in the necessity of some form of united nations organ-

[4] P. 226, Scribners.

ization or of world government. The Church should undergird and strengthen the principles and goals underlying such movements and is attempting to do so. But there is something incongruous and even absurd in the Church's preaching unity to the nations when they cannot set the example within their own fellowship. The obvious answer is "Physician, heal thyself." There is no reality in the Church's denouncing the factors which make up our broken world until they have come sincerely and courageously to grips with the same divisions among themselves. The plain truth is that the Church is unable to make a deep impress upon nations, officialdom of every degree or even upon the average person, the mythical man in the street who perhaps ought to understand what it is all about but seldom does.

But of course the supreme reason for a united Church is to be found in the will of Christ. He established a fellowship. In the *Book of Common Prayer* in the Collect for Good Friday we ask God "to behold this thy family, for which our Lord Jesus Christ was contented to be betrayed, and given up into the hands of wicked men, and to suffer death upon the cross." The Churches should be God's family in unity of spirit and of life. The divided Church not only is inefficient and lacking in force and example; it is a denial of the truth of unity in Christ. Yet all the time the reason given for the existing differences is loyalty to Christ. It is this fact which should work the deepest contrition in the hearts and minds of Christian men and women. There is much pious talk of this but there has not been sufficient repentance to move the Churches to direct and concrete action. This goes far to explain why the Churches have not been more effective agents of God in the terrible events of our time.

I realize as well as you do that I have over-simplified the problem if not the situation which exists. There are complicated movements and developments of history—great differences to be understood and to be reconciled. A strong and deeply Christian united Church of power cannot evolve out of communions which possess no depth and strength of conviction. It does not make for progress to deny this reality. There are many who see no difficulties in the way of reunion. The Quakers are an illustration of this. If one does not believe in creeds or in sacraments or in an historic Church, then differences in these matters seem to be unreal and beside the point. It is easy to dismiss the convictions of others when we do not share them. If we did not have any convictions about anything, then we could have a united Church tomorrow—but it would be difficult to know for what truths such a Church would be able and willing to witness. It will not do to underestimate the tremendous difficulties of the problem, for these cannot be solved by ignoring their existence or by underestimating their inherent power. It is not my purpose in this book to discuss Christian unity except as the facts reveal the present condition of the Christian Church. The plain truth is that a divided Church, whatever the reasons in the past and in the present, is a fundamental weakness in our witness to God in a broken and disordered world.

The Churches face many and powerful adversaries but that has always been true in every age. The greatest dangers we face as Christians are not from without but from within. If the fellowship of the Church could clearly and heroically manifest the mind and the spirit of Christ, then there would be no question as to the impress which would be made upon our so-called civilization. The influence of the Church is limited because clergy and people, take it by and large, are very fallible human beings. (In one sense this is as it should be.) The Church is not an organization of proved saints, a kind of ecclesiastical club of the self-righteous. The Church is made up of a very large constituency from every walk of life, the good and the not-so-good, the rich and the poor, those who follow the Master and reveal themselves in all that they are as of the company who have been with Jesus, and others who like St. Peter before the Crucifixion, follow him afar off, and some apparently not at all. As we shall see one of the thrilling opportunities before us is to mold this vast concourse of people into the Body of the Christ who lived and died that he might draw all men unto himself. Anything less than total humanity within the Church would be indeed a limited and narrow brotherhood. But this very fact makes the achievement of high purpose exceedingly difficult. Within the life of the Church, as in the world, it is the few who have caught the vision who are willing to bear the heat and burden of the day and who are truly attempting to live the Christ life. I have had a medium-sized parish and a large church. These past seventeen years I have had the opportunity to observe many parishes of various communions. The evidence is always the same. It is the few upon whom the life and work of the Church depends. This is not to say that the Church does not help many outside of this number. There are cares, pleasures, riches, burdens which seem to make poor ground in which the seed may grow. Any clergyman will do well to recognize this simple fact—else he will beat his wings against the cage to no effect. Numbers, buildings, organizations, budgets—these have their place. But these are of small effect compared to the company of faithful people. But the matter is more complicated even than this. Among the company of the faithful will be found many who with all their earnestness are small-minded and exceedingly difficult as fellow workers. I have often said that the chief fault to be found with devoted Church people is not that some of them are downright wicked, it is that they are so petty in their outlook. We need to remind ourselves again and again that Christ was crucified in large measure by the respectable, narrow Church people of his time. So we are faced by the reality that here at home in the United States, at least one half the population has no connection with any form of the Church; that of the half who are at least nominal members, only a small portion have really grasped the meaning of Christian discipleship, and that many of these, including perhaps ourselves, present peculiar personalities and problems.

These truths go far to explain the inability of the Churches to influence more powerfully the social order in which we are placed. The difficulty is that we are not able to mobilize the potential strength of the Churches. As I have said the weakness is not so much without as within. It was this nominal Christianity which so stirred the reproach and the irony of Kierkegaard. He wrote, "By indifferentism one commonly understands having no religion at all. But resolutely and definitely to have no religion at all is something passionate and so is not the most dangerous sort of indifferentism. Hence too it occurs rather rarely.

"No the most dangerous sort of indifferentism and the most common is to have a particular religion which is watered down and garbled into mere twaddle so that one can hold this religion in a perfectly passionateless way. That is the most dangerous sort of indifferentism; for precisely by having this trumpery under the name of religion, a person, so he thinks, is secured, made inaccessible against the reproach of having no religion." [5] Again he wrote, "But the truth is that not only are we not Christians but we are not so much as pagans to whom the Christian doctrine could be preached without embarrassment but by an illusion, a monstrous illusion, Christendom, a Christian state, a Christian land, a Christian world, we are even prevented from being as receptive as the pagans were." [6] These words have a modern ring. There are so many of us who feel ourselves to be Christians without the slightest understanding, or even effort at understanding, of the implications of what it means to be a disciple of Jesus Christ. We deceive ourselves by using great phrases and words,

[5] *Attack upon Christendom*, p. 185, Princeton University Press.
[6] *Ibid.*, p. 139.

particularly in our hymns—yet all the time we are literally playing with Christianity. The miracle on the whole is that the Church and Christianity are still vital in our world, considering the minimum of prayer, of sacrifice, of consecration we give to the task. This sounds pessimistic and discouraging but before we can improve we must have the courage to face the realities as they are.

When we consider what Christ demanded of his disciples it must be clear that we are indeed playing with Christianity. Among those listed as members of the Church may be found tremendous resources of intelligence, ability and financial means. These men and women are leaders in every field of activity in private and public affairs. Yet in general these resources are not devoted to the life and work of the Church. Somehow organized Christianity has failed to stir their imagination or their efforts. They will reveal wide vision in industry or professional life or community enterprises, yet when the Church is involved, they will either be indifferent or intensely parochial.

There are many illustrations of this. Let us take the vital problem of religious education. All of our chaplains, returned from service, agree that this is one of the Church's most patent failures. The average lay man or woman has little knowledge of the history,

41

or the content of the Christian Faith. Even the simplest facts of the life of Christ are unknown. Part of the responsibility for this condition rests upon the fact that in general we have had in Protestantism an exhorting, rather than a teaching ministry. It is, I believe, the exceptional preacher who is able to teach fundamental truths in a simple and appealing manner. The difficulty too lies with our Sunday schools. I realize full well all the attention given to this subject in theological seminaries, and that there are many excellent schools. But taking all the parishes in consideration the total picture is pathetic. As compared with public and private school instruction, the effort of the Church is thoroughly inadequate in amount of time available, in equipment, in support and interest of the home and in the personnel of the teaching force. There are, of course, thousands of effective teachers, but they are small in relation to the need. Any parish clergyman knows the extreme difficulty of enrolling the best trained men and women for Church work of this character. We generally starve our Sunday schools, which in many cases are dependent for support upon the gifts of the children themselves. We are playing with religious education and are not mobilizing the available resources of the Church. But of course the major responsibility for the present unhappy condition rests upon the home. The families in which there are prayers, reading the Bible, intelligent and serious discussion of matters pertaining to religion, are the exception rather than the rule. Even the most perfect of Sunday schools cannot overcome this spiritual lack in the home, and we cannot claim anywhere any kind of perfection in our schools. The trouble is that we are not taking Christianity seriously, and we are paying the price in a religiously illiterate generation. No amount of emotion can take the place of the consecration of the mind.

The inadequacy of our conception of the work of the Church is revealed in the failure to enlist the best men for the ministry and the failure to maintain adequate theological education and to support the ministry when the men have been trained. Again I am entirely aware that there are excellent men in the ministry and that there are splendid seminaries which stand on a par with the best education in any university department—but this does not change the general picture. The professions other than the ministry, those of medicine, law, industry, science, statesmanship, public service, appeal to the great majority of college men as of more significance and strategic importance than does the ministry. This is a reflection as to the state of the Church but more particularly it is again an indication as to the spiritual life in the home. Fathers and mothers do not long to have their sons enter the ministry—in certain cases they use every means to dissuade them. Thus the Churches are deprived of the best leadership.

Theological seminaries are crucial for the life of the Church for here men are prepared by study, discipline, prayer and fellowship for the work of the ministry. The key need of the Church is that of trained and consecrated personnel. Given the right man, results inevitably happen. Yet here is a field unknown in general even to interested and devoted lay people. There are notable theological centers of learning and of training, but they are few compared to the number of institutions struggling with poor equipment, inadequate support and underpaid staffs. Here once more is an indication that we are not applying intelligence to the life and work of the Church.

We have referred to the statistics of Church support. In one way Church contributions are not a reliable index to the state of the Church. In another way they are most revealing—for here in a realistic sense we can measure how much our Church people truly care and how much they are willing to sacrifice for the cause. Any pastor of a Church can, by looking through the list of contributors and the amount of contributions, gain a clear impression of the progress which is being made. For let us be honest, money counts heavily in our lives. It is not only revealing in the way we make it but equally so in the way we spend our incomes. I have been uplifted again and again by the sacrifice of men and women who have given small but generous sums out of no margin of safety whatever. There have been many notable benefactions on the part of people of large means but this is the exception again rather than the rule. Throughout the country clerical salaries, Church plants and equipment, missionary support are woefully inadequate. The wonder is that so much is accomplished with so little. I would not have men entering the ministry because it supplied a comfortable living—and the best men who are ordained never consider the economic picture—but it is disheartening to be forced to make bricks without straw, to be asked to achieve results without being given the necessary tools. These resources are available for industry, for science, for pleasure. But somehow we have not been able to capture the imagination of even interested people so that they understand the tremendous strategic significance of Christianity and the overwhelming claim of Christ to all that they are and have. The fault is not alone with these people. Christianity has not seemed to them important because we have failed to make it so. The ultimate answer is not to be found in more fervent and scolding appeals for funds, but in the character of the Christian community.

Here again we are given pause. How serious is the practice of the Christian life? We have seen that in the nation there are many evils to be overcome. Are the people who make up our Churches lights in the midst of contemporary darkness? In our cities and in many of our rural districts there are degrading slums. How conscious of these facts are our Church people to the point of doing something about them? In our communities there are lynchings, unfair practices, discrimination of the worst character. The laws, the principles, upon which our nation was founded are clear on these points. But even clearer are the teachings of the Master himself. Can we say that the members of our Churches in many cases do not share and do not perpetuate these practices and these prejudices? That would be indeed an impossible presupposition. There are again individual Christians, as there always have been, of vision and courage. But I am talking now of the general level of Church life and practice. It is clearly evident that the Church all too often simply accepts and reflects the standards, or the lack of standards, of the community. Thus we see in the Church the weakness and the limitation so evident at the present time in our total culture. As we think of the Church as the Body of Christ, the fellowship of heroic and faithful disciples of the Master, and then of the present Church, there can be no reason for complacency and self-congratulation.

I have had in mind non-Roman Catholic Christianity, but I do not believe that conditions are notably different within the Roman Catholic Church. They have a definite unity, they seldom criticize one another or the Church in public. There exists a kind of iron curtain. They make a great display of power which impresses many people and for this they verily have their reward. But when we come to the inner spiritual realities the same conditions we have described exist and are a matter of deep concern to those who care for the spiritual as against the material or political welfare of the Church. When I visited chaplains abroad the same reaction was observed from Roman Catholic as from other chaplains. Admittedly Roman Catholics performed more public, outward acts, their faith in that sense meant much to them. But no one, I think, could claim without prejudice that Roman Catholics were more truly Christian in the broadest sense of that term than the members of other Communions. In reality we are faced within all the Churches with that same sickness which afflicts all mankind in our day.

Once again I fully realize that I have made a one-sided, if not extreme, presentation of the present situation. Let me repeat that I know that there are many thousands of devoted clergymen giving their lives in the splendid service of God and their fellow men, that there are millions of consecrated men, women, boys, and girls who are consecrated disciples of the Master and that there are many parishes, small and large, which reveal in large measure the true spirit of Christian fellowship. All these are a leaven and a light. They prove the truth and the reality of Christian living and of Christian faith. But still it is true that they are the few rather than the many and that they are held back not so much by opposition of the wicked but by the inertia of the nominal and the indifferent.

The Church has made notable forward progress in certain activities and fields. Dr. Kenneth S. Latourette has chronicled the amazing development of Christian missions, particularly in the last one hundred years. Today there are few places in the world where there are not to be found representatives of the Christian Churches serving in evangelistic stations, schools and hospitals. The one world accepted as a political necessity today has always been a reality to the Christian missionary. No words can adequately describe the vision and the spirit of these men and women. But again it is the few who truly labor and care. I speak as one responsible for missionary administration. In our missionary endeavors we still meet the familiar phrase, "I do not believe in missions," even in the face of the evident facts of our world. We still face an overwhelming opportunity in countries like China and India with a shortage of workers and a minimum of support. With all the encouragement which we are entitled to receive from great accomplishment, we cannot fail to think what could be accomplished for the spread of the Gospel of Christ, for the peace and the spiritual well being of the world if we could only mobilize all our available resources of personnel and of money.

Another great reason for encouragement may be found in the growth of the Ecumenical Movement which has made such significant progress within the past forty years. Dr. William Adams Brown has told the story in detail in his book, *Toward a United Church*. In this book he traced the development of Church cooperation through the great conferences at Edinburgh, Stockholm, Oxford, Lausanne, Jerusalem, Madras, and others of less importance—all leading to the first meeting of the World Council of Churches in Holland in the summer of 1948. To name the geographical places of meeting is to stress the world-wide character of the movement. Here have come representatives of the East and the West,

of many differing points of view, to worship and to
reason together in the effort to express in the life of
the Churches and of the world a common loyalty to
God as He is revealed in Christ. Dr. Brown enumer-
ated the old factors in the movement—a common
faith, the same Bible, many of the same prayers and
hymns and a common ethical ideal. The new factor
he described as the effort to "apply the spirit of the
thirteenth chapter of 1st Corinthians to every phrase
of the Church's institutional life." He continued, "The
Churches which unite in the Movement do not claim
for themselves an exclusive possession of true Christianity. They recognize that others also possess truths
which they themselves have not always cherished as
they should. They come to the conference table,
therefore, not only as teachers but as learners, eager
not only to give but—what is often harder—to receive.
Thus, they are trying, so far as it is possible for representatives of institutions, to apply to their life as
Churches the Pauline principle of love and they are
finding to their surprise that the key that makes
possible fellowship between persons is not less effective in opening the door to institutional fellowship.
This association of Churches, which differ in their
understanding of God's Will for His Church, in common worship, common work, and common study is

something new in Christian history." [7] This emphasis upon Christian love has been even more marked in the post-war world since Dr. Brown's death. Today with headquarters in Europe and in the Far East, representatives of many Christian Churches are engaged in dispensing relief, in rebuilding the spiritual life in many devastated countries, using funds contributed by countless Christians of numerous Churches. Here is the spirit of Christ at work in our stricken world. Barriers between nations and peoples are broken down in understanding and helpful service. In addition those who are cooperating in this work are learning to know one another and to appreciate as never before the unity which already exists in the family of Christ.

In this country the Federal Council of Churches has made encouraging progress as the number of the participating Churches has increased and the program of cooperative effort has widened and deepened. The biennial meetings of the Federal Council have a great inspirational value and they also serve to bring to bear upon society the impress of the Christian Evangel. In between these sessions, there are others of importance having to do with many fields. For example, the Commission on a Just and Durable Peace exerted great influence in the genesis

[7] P. 11, Scribners.

of the United Nations. It is impossible to over-emphasize the importance of the Federal Council in our American Christianity, not only for what is said and done but because here is a meeting place where those of varying points of view and traditions can learn confidence and trust in one another.

Beyond any question all of this new spirit of co-operation is encouraging. There does seem to be a new and a better temper. If there were all the time in the world available, we could look forward with confidence to steady development. But we must not forget that we are living in an atomic age, essentially upon borrowed time. Even now nations are in the race to develop new weapons of destruction. The course of these post-war years does not give promise that men have learned the ways of peace even in the crucible of war. We are saying continually that the forces of the Spirit are the only possible answer to the needs of our time but we move so pathetically and slowly toward the effective means of applying those forces to the world in general. In the light of this fact the united witness of the Churches leaves much to be desired. The World Council of Churches is still largely an ideal held by many of the leaders of the Churches.[8] It has not yet touched the lives of

[8] Note. The World Council of Churches became a reality in Amsterdam in August 1948. For this great step forward we may thank God, but this fact makes *only* a first step.

the overwhelming majority of clergy and of laity. This whole movement must be brought to the parochial level in a great program of education. On the one hand we must promote this ideal in every possible way, by every means of popular education and of enthusiastic support. On the other hand there is danger that we give the impression that we have already reached an objective which is in reality still far distant. Because there is an increase of cooperation, because 1948 marked the first meeting of a World Council, does not mean we can rest back and be content with the situation which is not unlike that of the United Nations which, although established, must prove its power.

As we conclude this survey of the Church situation, I find myself between two extremes. On the one hand there are those who would denounce contemporary Christianity with the bitterness of a Kierkegaard's criticism of the formal state Christianity of his time. When I am tempted to do this, and it is not difficult to do, I think of the spiritual life and vitality revealed in the lives of so many. I am reminded of a remark of Basil King's which I have remembered many years. "The Church is that institution which has kept the divine light aglow in a world which otherwise would have blown it out." That statement could be defended in the past. With all our manifold failures and weaknesses it is true today. In a world desperately trying to blow out the divine light, the Christ Life in men and women in the Churches stands as a beacon of hope. On the other hand I find myself unsympathetic with those who either wittingly or unwittingly are blind to the facts and who feel it necessary in loyalty to their calling to be over-optimistic in sermon and address and in attitude as to the present situation of the Churches. We must beware of both despair and of complacency. We should face realities without fear, with open eyes— and with faith in the power and the love of the God who has called the Churches and each one of us to His service.

# III

## *IF GOD BE FOR US*

IN THE two preceding chapters we have attempted to estimate the present situation which confronts the Christian Churches. There are many, no doubt, who will feel that I have over-emphasized the weaknesses of the Churches and have correspondingly exaggerated the difficulties to be overcome. In a world in which men in general have tended to depreciate the Churches, it may be said that the first task is to testify to their undoubted strength and significance and that there are sufficient numbers outside of the Christian fellowship who can point out our failures. It should hardly be necessary for me to state my faith in the mission of the Christian Church. Without that faith I should not be in the ministry. But I do feel that there is nothing to be gained by an unreal optimism. As I have said previously—the great danger the Churches face is that of a surprising, in the light of the world situation, complacency on the part of many Church leaders and a large part of the lay constituency of the

Churches—a complacency which is revealed in our failure to make determined, sacrificial and daring adventures in the name of God. We do not as yet comprehend the urgency of our times. If we did, much more would be happening in Church assemblies, parishes, and congregations, in the personal life of each one of us. We must beware, of course, of the opposite danger of frustration, that men will become discouraged and say, "We are in the midst of such tremendous world forces that there is nothing we can do to redeem the situation one way or another." The answer to that is faith in the living God as revealed in Christ. The source of hope is not found in the listing of our own somewhat meagre achievements as Christians but in the purpose and character of the everlasting God we worship and are pledged to serve.

There are many responsibilities and opportunities which confront the Churches. But the most vital and significant of them all is to testify to the reality of the living God. In a world of space and of time, in which men are easily led astray by the transitory and the insignificant, the Church's chief task is to state in words and in life that the righteous God lives, rules and loves. Here is the deepest truth of religion and one which runs like a golden thread through all of man's experience of God. It is expressed in the Old Testament again and again in the conviction that the Jewish nation was called by God. In the New Testament is found the same emphasis—"Ye have not chosen me. I have chosen you." In the *Book of Common Prayer,* the Collects have many phrases such as "O God, forasmuch as without thee we are not able to please thee." The Roman Catholic, Baron von Hugel writes, "Careful research, severe criticism, daring hypothesis, independence from aught but the laws and tests found to be absolutely intrinsic to the respective ranges and levels of study, will be needful as ever; but all will now move within a frank recognition of Givenness, of Otherness, of Reality. Our minds will now range from the givenness of the pebble and the star to the givenness of the lichen, of the bee and the bird, on to the immensely greater givenness of the human spirit and (contrasting with, yet sustaining all such givennesses and their numberless given real inter-relations) the primary, absolute givenness and Reality of God." [1] Von Hugel writes of Troeltsch, "No living thinker has so much as Troeltsch insisted upon the sense of givenness and of otherness as characteristic of all genuine religion and no one has better analyzed and described this evidential charac-

---

[1] Baron Frederick von Hugel, *Essays and Addresses* (First Series), p. 190, E. P. Dutton & Co., Inc., N. Y.

ter of all religions, or has more clearly shown how only the acceptance of this evidence as true and final brings formness, inter-connection and sufficient rationality into our life as a whole and depth in all its parts." [2] A. E. Taylor declares, "To be quite plain, in all moral advance the ultimate 'efficient cause' must be the real eternal source of both becoming and value. The initiative in the process of 'assimilation to God' must come from the side of the eternal; it must be God who first comes to meet us, and who all through the moral life itself 'works in us' in a sense which is more than metaphorical. Our moral endeavors must be genuinely ours but they must be responses to intimate actual contacts in which a real God moves outward to meet His creatures, and by the contact at once sustains and inspires the appropriate response on the creature's part." [3]

This point of view so inherent in the Gospel of Christ and in Christian thinking through all the succeeding ages might be taken for granted, were it not that it has been so consistently denied in our modern world. We have been interested largely, to the exclusion of God, in man as man—so that extremely critical of the simplicity of anthropomorphism, we have been even more naive in giving to

[2] *Ibid.*, p. 187.
[3] *Faith of a Moralist*, I, p. 223, Macmillan. Used by permission.

man the attributes of God. Part of the shock of the present comes from the stern realization of the failure of that very man, in whom we had built up such overwhelming faith. Religion has been described purely in terms of humanity, for this type of secularism has penetrated Christian thinking under the name of religious humanism. This was once described in a conversation with me by Dr. Francis G. Peabody, that staunch old Unitarian, "as the greatest religious illiteracy of the age." A great deal of emphasis has been made upon religion as being purely wishful thinking. It is claimed that people find themselves unable to meet the tasks of life by themselves, so they build up a dream world of God and Eternity as a retreat from life. That there has been this misuse of religion must be readily admitted. But any description of religion as wishful thinking ignores the fact that religion at the best has been just the opposite. The prophets faced suffering and persecution because they were true to what they conceived to be the stern demands of God's Will. St. Paul declared, "Necessity is laid upon me. Woe is unto me if I preach not the gospel." Martin Luther cried, "God helping me I can do no other." The central truth of Christianity has to do with the hard acceptance of death upon the Cross in obedience to the Will of God. True Christianity, far from being "wishful thinking" has seen men and women bear heavy burdens, overcome great obstacles, with complete personal sacrifice in loyalty to the objective demand of faith in the living God.

"Life," according to Herbert Spencer, "is an adjustment of internal relations to external relations." If there be no real external relationship to which to adjust, then we are of all men most miserable, the very substance of all that has been meant by Christian faith has disappeared into vague generalities. There is a story I have heard attributed to Mark Twain. He was asked if he were going to hear Robert G. Ingersoll lecture on the "Mistakes of Moses." He replied that he would not pay five cents to hear Mr. Ingersoll lecture on "The Mistakes of Moses," but that he would pay a great deal if he could only hear Moses lecture on "The Mistakes of Robert G. Ingersoll." We have been looking through the wrong end of the telescope. We have concerned ourselves with discussions as to whether we approve of God and of His ways, whereas the important thing is what is God's judgment upon our world and upon our lives. The Church's task has to do with ethics as well as with what Bishop Brent described as "ambulance work," the caring for the desolate, the destitute, the forlorn. But the essential difference between the Church and an Ethical Culture or a Family

Welfare Society is that the Church's ministry must be shot through and through with the conviction of the presence, the power and the redeeming love of God. The world can have no real unity simply through political processes. We must learn a deeper truth, that we are members one of another because we are the children of a common Father. The world needs a conception of the validity of a universal moral law. This will not be accomplished by trials and punishments in the name of such a law, but only as men come to believe in a supreme Law Giver whose service is perfect freedom.

This primacy of God is vital to every aspect of the life of the Christian Church. In the Ordinal of the *Book of Common Prayer,* the Ordinand is asked, "Do you think that you are truly called to this ministry?" The initiative is from God in Christ. The Christian minister administers the sacraments, preaches the gospel, makes parish calls, serves, advises, by the nature of that call. Karl Barth has a moving passage in his book, *The Word of God and The Word of Man:* "On Sunday morning when the bells ring to call the congregation and members to Church, there is in the air an expectancy that something great, crucial and even momentous is to happen. How strong the expectancy is in the people who are interested, or even whether there are any people

who are interested or even whether there are any people whatever who consciously cherish it, is not our
question now. Expectancy is inherent in the whole
situation." [4] Then after some words about the institution of the Church he writes: "And here above all
is a man upon whom the expectation of the apparently imminent event seems to rest in a special way.
And now before the congregation and for the congregation he will pray—you note—pray to God. He
will open the Bible and read from it words of infinite import, words that refer all of them to God.
And then he will enter the pulpit and here is daring!
Preach. Everyone must apparently, perhaps *nolens
volens,* speak of God. And then the man will have the
congregation sing ancient songs full of weighty and
weird memories, strange ghostly witnesses of the
sufferings, struggles and triumphs of the long-de-
parted fathers, all leading to the edge of an immeas-
ureable event, all whether the minister and people
understand what they are saying or not, full of rem-
iniscences of God, always of God." [5] God is present.
"God is present." The whole situation witnesses,
cries, simply shouts of it even when in minister or
people there arises questionings or wretchedness or
despair. Then perhaps it is witnessed to best of all,

[4] Pp. 104-106, Copyright, The Pilgrim Press. Used by permission.
[5] *Ibid.*

62

better than when the real problem is obscured or concealed by abundant human success. I have quoted at some length because this passage has stayed by me for many years. At a service I think that something "great and crucial" is to happen. There is "an expectancy in the air." Many times in visiting some small mission congregation for confirmation, with three or four to be confirmed, I have learned that God is present "when the real problem is" not "obscured or concealed by abundant human success."

The Church can only meet the problems and the perplexities of this rapidly changing world order by a deepened conviction and experience of God, who is infinitely more than the product of our hopes and desires. He is the God, not alone of the Churches, but of all life,—to quote again von Hugel, "of the lichen, of the bee, and the birds and of the human spirit." He is the God not only of nature but is found in the processes of history, yes, in the confused tensions and events of this very hour. As the prophets of old saw the purpose and the judgment of God in the course of nations such as Assyria and Egypt, so we should be trying to read the signs of God's presence and will in the United States, the China, and the Russia of today.

We must not forget that there is an otherness about God—just because He is the Creator and the initiative is in His hands. We may be grateful for the revelation of God in Christ as a loving Father with whom we are able to have communion. But there is another essential element—that of awe so eloquently described by Rudolf Otto in his *Idea of the Holy*. At the risk of being old fashioned, I am willing to assert that the fear of the Lord is still the beginning, if not the end of wisdom. In our own lives with our smallness of vision, we cannot hope to make our ways His. Our faith cannot be true faith if it is dependent upon the success of our prayers, our efforts and programs, even the survival of our civilization. "Yea though he slay me, yet will I believe in him."

The supreme reality is God. All else is secondary because derived. All of life is a means toward God. Our tendency always is to make these means ends in themselves. The Church, the sacraments, the ministry are only valid as they are viewed as pathways to God. Even the historic Christ in one aspect must be viewed in this light. It is "through Jesus Christ our Lord" that we pray to the eternal God.

The chief contribution of the Christian Churches in these days of uncertainty and of trial will be to serve as meeting places between God and man. That fact, if true, demands a re-examination of our practices, our services, the quality of the spiritual life of clergy and of laity. I do not mean that the Churches are to be ecclesiastical dugouts into which men and women can go to escape from life. Rather they should be powerhouses to send people out into life with new courage, purpose and vision. Certainly it is true, despite the recognized growth of secularism, that there are millions of people longing with poignant eagerness for a reality, deeper and greater than they are. They are the sheep led astray and yet pathetically eager to be fed. Dr. Fosdick in a magazine article declares that there are 4011 accredited psychiatrists in this country and that as we all know they are swamped. [6] Of course, as he states, the psychiatrist serves an important and essential function. But he goes on to say, "Nothing would do more to keep people from needing the help of psychiatrists than a renewal of intelligent, vital, personal religion. I am talking here solely about religious essence—establishing in human hearts in this harassed world an inner sanctuary where tranquility abides, driving out grudges, bearing hatreds with magnanimous goodwill, cleansing the soul of unforgiveness and opening doors of help to self-accusing consciences, releasing life from its egocentricity into worthwhile endeavor to 'make the most of our best for the sake

[6] *Reader's Digest*, "How to Keep Out of the Psychiatrists' Hands," July, 1947.

of others,' substituting for blighting sarcasm a victorious faith in life's eternal meaning and purposefulness, and supplying interior resources to meet life's strains." What he is saying in more popular terms is that these men and women need God.

Are our Churches meeting this primary need? Of course they are in many respects but I find myself thinking of poorly planned and conducted services, of liturgies carelessly or conventionally read, of pastoral prayers which have little reverence because they tell God so many things He doubtless knows already. I find myself thinking of anthems in which the choirmaster and the choir are more evident than the worship of God, of sermons in which the desire of the clergyman to attract or to entertain crowds or to expound his own notions and theories is clearer than the preaching of the Word of God. I am thinking of congregations to which not everyone is welcome, and whose atmosphere belies the spirit of fellowship within the Church. "The Lord is in his holy temple." Were that truth made more manifest, the Churches would be more nearly performing their primary function.

I am not pleading necessarily for more ritual. Certainly there has been a marked increase in this regard in all Churches. Those who are members of liturgical Churches tend to rejoice. I have some reservations. I trust that my own liturgical brethren will not object to a comment by the way. Perhaps because of my congregational forebears I have been moved many times by the very austerity of worship in the simplicity of the tradition of our Puritan ancestors. Here is one aspect of true worship in spirit and in truth. Ritual whatever it may be must have meaning. There is also in ritual an historical significance. When ritual is introduced without regard to either of these factors, the result is not helpful. My point is that the worship of God must express the most definite conviction and the most careful thought and preparation. Ritual, and there must be some in every Church, whatever our background, may be a pathway to God or it may deserve all the uncomplimentary remarks made so often by the prophets.

But this is an aside. The point I would stress again and again is that the Church by her very commission, in all of her worship and work, stands first and foremost for God, for that eternal life which alone makes all our own lives significant. If God be for us, who can be against us? The times may be difficult, the future uncertain and unknown. In Him we find courage and everlasting hope.

In the faith of the Christian Church, God is no mere First Cause, unknown and unknowable. He is incomprehensibly greater than our own understanding, our experience and our ability of expression. But the heart of Christianity is to believe in the clearest evidence of God's initiative. "God so loved the world that he gave . . . ." We discuss the question of the divinity of Christ as if we knew all about God, and we debate whether Jesus is divine. But the deepest meaning of the Incarnation is to see Jesus as he was in history, full of grace and truth and to say that here is an answer to the most vital of all questions, the character of the eternal God, Creator and Source of all life. "He that hath seen me hath seen the Father." Dean Inge has said that the gospel is not so much good advice as we are so prone to make it, but good news. It is the proclamation of good news of many kinds, of the resurrection of Christ, of the possibilities within humanity, but primarily it is good news of God. In relation to Christ's mission, we have again that question of emphasis as between God and Man. Was Jesus the product of humanity? Can we look at him and say, "Behold what has been produced by the forces of evolution?" Is he the outreach of man toward God? Or is he the gift of God to the children of men, God's redeeming love seeking as the Good Shepherd in the Master's Parable the lost sheep? I realize of course that the communion between God and man must be two-sided. There must be man's response.

One cannot stress the divine in Jesus without by necessity emphasizing his humanity. The Church has historically considered as heretical the elimination of either the human or the divine. It sounds orthodox to declare that "Jesus is God" or otherwise to say that "Jesus is Man." Each is incomplete without the other. In certain ages the Church has lost the fullness of truth by over-emphasizing one or the other aspect. What I am chiefly concerned with here is that Jesus is the supreme example of God's redeeming initiative and love. The Church has the resource of the proclamation of this overwhelming "good news." Again as we view our world, we seem caught on a treadmill of prejudice, of fear and of error. We may well cry, "Who shall deliver us from the body of this death?" By ourselves we are unable to save ourselves. The gospel assures us of God's concern with our lives. The Church can proclaim, "Here is the way that leads unto Life."

It is important to realize that this faith is grounded in history. Dr. Reinhold Niebuhr has a striking sentence in his chapter in the book of tributes to the Reverend Henry Sloane Coffin: "Dr. Coffin spanned the period of American Protestant history in which the controversy between liberalism and fundamentalism broke out in full fury. This controversy was due to the fact that one part of the Church sought to protest the essential emphases of the Christian gospel by the armor of Christian obscurantism, while the other half of the Church sought so desperately achievements of a scientific era, that it frequently ended by sacrificing every characteristic Christian insight to the prejudices of a technically competent but culturally vapid age." [7] When I say that the Christian Faith is grounded in history, I do not mean the legalism or the obscurantism of fundamentalism which bears out the famous definition of "faith" as "believing things you know aren't so." During the past fifty years the Bible has been studied as never before in the light of every canon of scientific research. As a result the central facts of Christianity stand out in more certain focus. God's developing revelation of Himself in history is more clearly understood. On the other hand we who are not fundamentalists must beware of the other danger and extreme, "the sacrificing every characteristic Christian insight to the prejudices of a technically competent but culturally vapid age." It is the essential "givenness" of Christianity which alone can prevent this—the truth that we are dealing not with philosophical or theosophical theories but with the facts of history. To be sure there are areas and incidents of the past which will always be clouded with mystery. But in general

[7] *This Ministry*, p. 119, Scribners.

the figure and the teaching of the historic Christ
stand without reasonable question. The attempts of
certain so-called scholars to prove that Jesus is a
figment of the imagination have long since been
justifiably consigned to the realm of absurdity.

With the advent of the increased emphasis upon
the historic Christ, there have been movements which
have declared the necessity of going back to Jesus,
to what is considered to be the simplicity of his life
and teaching. Such a corrective is essential but it
must be understood that there are severe limitations
in this approach. Too often this means reading into
the message of Jesus our own prejudices and opinions, as if, someone has said, he lived in the twentieth
century in a democratic society and in a scientific
age. The comment has been made that looking at
Christ is like looking down a well in which we see
only our own reflection. There is an "otherness" in
Christ as well as an intimacy. The movement back
to Christ must not mean the transference of our point
of view to his times. Furthermore it is impossible
to by-pass almost two thousand years of the history
of the Christian Church in which men have thought
deeply about Christ. To quote Dr. T. R. Glover's
titles, we must not only know the *Jesus of History*
but *Jesus in the Experience of Men.* George Tyrrell
and some of those associated with him made the

mistake of minimizing the authority of the historic Jesus and over-emphasizing the theory of development which might as a result lead anywhere or nowhere. It would be an equal error to attempt to move from today to New Testament times without regard to the intervening centuries. Alfred Loisy was right at least when he wrote, "It is true that as a result of the evolution, political, intellectual, economic, of the modern world, as a result of all that may be called the modern spirit, a great religious crisis affecting Churches, orthodoxies and forms of worship has arisen to a greater or less extent everywhere. The best means of meeting it does not appear to be the suppression of all ecclesiastical organization, all orthodoxy, and all traditional worship—a process that would thrust Christianity out of life and humanity, but to take advantage of what is, in view of what should be, to repudiate nothing of the heritage left to our age by former Christian centuries, to recognize how necessary and useful is the immense development accomplished in the Church, to gather the fruits of it, and continue it since the adaptation of the Gospel to the changing conditions of humanity is as pressing as it ever was and ever will be." [8]

This importance of the historical aspect of Chris-

[8] *The Gospel and the Church*, p. 276, Scribners.

tianity and of the Church is of the utmost significance today when we face a rapidly changing world
order and when the currents of life are so confused
and confusing. In general we have been inclined to
use the word "modern" as an adjective of commen-
dation. The events of the present reveal the inadequacy and the shallowness of this approach by itself. We need the judgment and the experience of the
Christian generations. Every age has its limitations
and inadequacies. We are all of us necessarily subjective and we must have the breadth and the depth
of the objective. There is this vital element of the
"given" in Christ and in the Church. To be able to
interpret the gospel to a new day, there must be a
gospel. In the light of Christian history it is naive
to divorce the gospel from the fellowship of the
Church.

However in stressing the importance of the historical aspect of Christ and of Christianity, we must
not make the mistake of forgetting the significance
of the eternal. A false other-worldliness has at times
led Christians to disparage the meaning not only of
nature but of human history. Our own pressing danger of recent days has been to say one world at a
time. We have enough to do and to face here and
now without troubling about the future. It is not a
matter of either—or, but of both. Canon Charles E.

Raven in his book, *The Gospel and the Church,* quotes a statement of Archbishop Temple: "The eternal is the ground of the historical and not vice versa; but the relation is necessary not contingent— essential not incidental. In and through the forces of evolution, the rise and fall of dynasties, of nations, of civilizations, the countless decisions of generations of men, the Christian sees the unfolding of the will and the purpose of the eternal God. Because this is true and only so are these events and men significant. The Christian plays his part as best he may in the contemporary scene but he has no illusions as to earthly Utopias, and as to the finality of this world in which to a very real extent we are but strangers and sojourners." [9] Round and about him is eternal life—not alone as a future promise but as a present reality. It is this which gives him poise, vision and courage.

There have been those who have portrayed Jesus as a great hero, dying bravely in defeat and despair with the words on his lips, "My God, my God, why hast thou forsaken me?" But this interpretation, denying the historicity of the Resurrection stops far short of the Christian interpretation of all that Christ means to us. As Canon Raven states, "If in the person

[9] *The Gospel and the Church,* p. 214 (T. & T. Clark). Scribners.

of the Son of Man God 'has visited and redeemed his people' then the history of Israel as the New Testament claims and indeed the whole previous history of humanity as Justin and Origen insist are a preparation for that event. It must be seen as a moment—the culminating and illuminative moment in an age-old and worldwide drama, a drama in which nothing can be dismissed as irrelevant to it; as the characteristic and representative expression of principles inherent in the whole process of creation; as the criterion by which past and future are given their true significance. From it history derives its vital importance as recording not only the adventures of men but the self-manifestation of God." [10] It is the initiative of God. Jesus is the supreme sacrament in the midst of this transitory life with the ebb and the flow of human events.

So it is as we view the history of the Christian Church. It is possible to see, as did Gibbon and many others past and present, only in the Church the self-seeking of ambitious and contentious ecclesiastics. But that explanation ignores the reality of the continuing spiritual life of the Church apparent in the sacrifice and the service of innumerable men and women in every age to the present hour. You and I are under no illusion as to the failures of the

[10] *Ibid.*, p. 215.

Churches. Indeed we have already faced them to a somewhat discouraging degree. But when that has been said we also know by experience and conviction we have found within the Churches the presence of this living God who has vitally touched our lives. The Church again at the best is a sacrament.

Indeed all of life seen in the light of the eternal is sacramental. There is the inward grace of the spiritual in every outward and visible sign. But that does not preclude special manifestations of this grace. God is in a man in a different sense than in a tree. God is more evident in the saint than in the sinner. Of course God is present everywhere in his creation but, practically, that may mean to many people that he is nowhere. The Church has always held that there are special times and occasions when he may be found, as in Baptism and the Holy Communion, in which the outward and visible signs were common articles of daily use in the time of the Master and the early Church. These sacraments, as is the case with every gift of God, may be misused. They may become ends in themselves and limitations of God's free spirit. They have become causes of bitter misunderstanding and controversy. They have been used as weapons for ecclesiastical victory or as measures for discipline. But they also have brought the Spirit of God into the lives of countless followers

76

of the Christ. In the debates of philosophers, God to most men seems far off. But they can find God in the Master who overcame temptation, who faced opposition, and who steadfastly set his face to go to Jerusalem. So with many of us, dependent upon environment, swayed by moods, it is not always easy to know God. There is an objectivity in the service and in the words "Do this." Our faith does not create the presence of God in the sacrament. He is there independent of us. It is again the givenness of God and it is for us to prepare our minds and hearts to receive and to respond. I am frank to say that in my own spiritual life I need this objectivity and this gift. It is finding "God in Christ" in this special place which makes his presence more real everywhere else and I find in this nothing strange, but a natural means of meeting God where He may be found.

The reason for the spiritual sickness of modern man is that his religion is vague, individualistic and undisciplined. At times of crisis he turns toward the Church. But at other times he likes to say that he finds God in the woods or in the reading of a good book at home. There are doubtless many who haply find God in nature and in their homes. I trust that we all do. But it is difficult to believe that the great majority who use those easy phrases find a deep spiritual experience. There are too many thousands confused by the events of today, strained beyond measure, yet longing for strength and courage. Here is the objectivity of God and yet the greatest simplicity of approach to make possible the manifold gifts of the Spirit. It is again God in history, a redeeming living God who in the incarnation, in the continued spiritual life of the Church, so loves the world.

Some one may say that all I have stated is well known, that it is the traditional emphasis of the historic Church. Some years ago Dr. Brander Matthews wrote: "In life, in literature, in all the arts we cannot fail to perceive an unwonted restlessness, an unprecedented distaste for balance or harmony and proportion accompanied by a desire to be different, by a seeking for novelty for its own sake, by a relish for eccentricity and freakness—by a refusal to profit by what has been bequeathed us by the past. In this new century we have been called upon to admire painting by men who have never learnt how to paint, dancing by women who have never learnt how to dance, verse by persons of both sexes who have never acquired the elements of versification."

This statement has its application to the field of religion. Here too there has been a desire to be different, a seeking for novelty for its own sake. We have had an era of the discussion group which often means the pooling of the ignorance of all concerned. It is characteristic of American life that while the average man feels in considerable awe of most experts, he feels himself perfectly able to discourse with authority upon the subject of religion. Of course the gospel must be applied in the language of today but all too often this has meant simply the expression of the mood and the fancies of the present without knowledge or depth. Before a gospel can be applied there must be a gospel—the good news. In this hour we have considered two vital elements in Christianity—the givenness of God and the redeeming love of God in Jesus Christ. Here may be found facts both of history and experience. Take any period in the history of the Christian Church when there has been evidenced spiritual power and these truths will be found to have been central. Without them Christianity has degenerated into sentimentality or weak acquiescence to the folk ways of contemporary life. We can never lift ourselves by our own boot straps nor can we meet the manifold problems of today merely by asking questions and having no answers. If Christianity be not true then no one of us should wish to go through the pretense of being Christian. But if these central realities are the truth then it is the power of God unto salvation. There are many disagreements and many grounds of question on the peripheries of the Christian faith and life. But these at the present are insignificant in comparison with the main issues of spiritual life and death. Men are longing for leadership and for guidance. They are eager for spiritual power and for vision. If we have convictions then let us not be ashamed of them. The entire fellowship of the Church, whatever our other differences may be, can unite in proclaiming with one voice that the omnipotent God reigneth, but more than this that in Christ he has shown his redeeming love. Here is the supreme fact which makes hope possible in our tragic era. Here may be found spiritual resources which can enable us to redeem our times. Here is the faith which the Master proclaimed. "Be of good cheer, I have overcome the world."

# IV

## THE MASTER AND THE FELLOWSHIP OF THE SPIRIT

WE HAVE been considering the resources of the Christian Church in facing the tasks of today. We have seen that the Church possesses the gifts of strength and of hope because of faith in a living and righteous God who is found in nature and in history and especially in the life, death and resurrection of Jesus Christ. It is this "givenness" of God which is of supreme importance. But in Jesus we see not alone the divine reaching out to man but as well the perfect response to the divine Will. The human aspect of Jesus' life is of the utmost significance. The Church has the great resource of the example and the teaching of the Master. It was this which in the first instance moved the early disciples. Attracted by all that he was, they lived with him, heard him teach and in that companionship, with all their limitations of understanding and of courage, they were so changed that others took knowledge of them that they had been with Jesus. Only later was the Christian community able to find greater and eternal significance in the events of his life.

The humanity of Jesus has similarly made an appeal to men in every succeeding generation. His youth, the courage with which he faced opposition even to death on the Cross, his understanding of human nature, the depth of his compassion, his love of nature, the simplicity yet the profundity of his teaching in regard to God and man, his rejection of the letter and the minutiae of the Jewish law, his call for sacrificial and heroic action on the part of his followers—all this and much more have drawn disciples to him in every age. There has been an attempt to oversimplify the message and the life of the Christ by stressing a distinction between the religion *of* Jesus and the religion *about* Jesus. Of course there has been much said and written about Jesus which falls short of the truth. On the other hand the language of devotion has at times seemed to forget the reality of his human nature. But to press the contrast between the religion of and about Jesus would be equivalent to a demand that we stop thinking about him. The task of the historian is much greater than an enumeration of historic facts; he is forced to a consideration and discussion of their significance. The theologian must start with

82

facts but he must interpret these in the light of their relationship to God's dealing with men in the unfolding of His will and purpose. Nor is it possible to separate the religion and the ethics of Jesus. It is not enough as some have asserted to believe in the Golden Rule, or in the commandment, "Thou shalt love thy neighbor," without a realization that there was also the first and great commandment, "Thou shalt love the Lord thy God." Without this first commandment it is impossible to understand Jesus' references to the Kingdom which was not of men but of God, the application of many of the parables, and the sternness with which he set forth goals impossible of accomplishment by men alone. The attempt of modern man to divorce religion and ethics is one reason for our present spiritual and moral sickness. In the long run ideals cannot survive loss of faith in the living God. The Master in his teaching assumed this faith. His ethics were the product of his perfect communion with God. The Church has the privilege of proclaiming the good news of God but also of setting forth the example and the teaching of him who living among men, tempted as we all are, nevertheless overcame the world.

The Master taught the eternal worth of human personality because men are the children of God. It

seems unnecessary to prove this, the fact is so patent in many of the parables such as that of the
Lost Sheep, in the Sermon on the Mount, indeed in
the conduct of his entire ministry. "The very hairs
of your head are numbered." "Are ye not much more
than many sparrows?" "What profiteth a man if he
gain the whole world and lose his own soul?" "Forasmuch as ye have done it unto one of the least of
these, my brethren, ye have done it unto me." With
Jesus once again the emphasis is from above. Righteousness, eternal life, human worth are the gifts of
God. Ernst Troeltsch in his *Social Teaching of the
Christian Churches* in his discussion of the gospel
ethic declares, "The first outstanding characteristic
is an unlimited, unqualified individualism. The
standard of this individualism is wholly self-con-
tained, determined simply by its own sense of that
which will further its consecration to God. It is
bound to go all lengths in obedience to the demands
of the Gospel. Its basis and its justification lie in
the fact that man is called to fellowship with God
and in the eternal relationship which this filial relationship confers. The individual as a child of God
may regard himself as infinitely precious but he
reaches this goal only through self-abnegation in
unconditional obedience to the Holy Will of God. It
is clear that an individualism of this kind is entirely

radical and that it transcends all mutual barriers and differences through the ideal of the religious value of the soul. It is also clear that such an individualism is only possible at all upon this religious basis." [1]

With this emphasis upon the individual, the Master taught a universalism. "I, if I be lifted up will draw all men unto me," is an accurate description of his purpose. The parable of the Good Samaritan is an illustration and even more his own practice in breaking down the barrier between Jew and Samaritan. Troeltsch writes: "Thus out of an absolute individualism there arises a universalism which is equally absolute. Both these aspects of the Gospel are based entirely upon religion; their support is the thought of the Holy Divine Will of Love and they mutually aid each other quite logically." [2]

Among the many principles taught by Jesus, these two, individualism and universalism are peculiarly germane to the conditions and the needs of our time. The great issue in the political world is between democracy and totalitarian regimes whether to the right or to the left. Democracy at its best is based upon the worth of the individual. The Hitler and Mussolini governments regarded human per-

[1] Vol. I, p. 55, Tr. Wyon, Macmillan. Used by permission.
[2] *Ibid.*, p. 57.

sonality with ruthless cynicism as evidenced by innumerable acts, the suppression of free popular choice, the concentration camps and the cruel sacrifice of human life. Many of these same conditions appear to exist in Soviet Russia as well as elsewhere in the world. Wherever the power of the State is used in this way, the Christian Church, if true to her Master must stand in opposition. In the mind of true Christians today an all powerful State cannot rightly claim the attributes of God any more than could the Roman emperors of the first century. Indeed as in the case of Rome, the worship of the State may become a religion with great mass gatherings, a certain ritual, and an ideology which in the case of the Nazis was an attempt to revive faith in the ancient and long forgotten gods. The gospel of Christ can never make terms with the all-powerful State placed above personality, even above God. But in taking this position we must beware of identifying self-righteously the will of God with our own practice of democracy. In our own country as well as in other democratic nations, there has been and is exploitation of men, women, boys and girls—as witness many of the disgraceful conditions which grew out of the industrial revolution, as well as the slums in city and country today, and the situation which exists in regard to various minority

86

groups in this country in the denial of civil rights, and of an equal opportunity for education. There are dangers to human personality even in democracies. Intolerant public opinion can exert devastating power. We are told on excellent authority that our failures to practice democracy at home make difficult the spread of the democratic spirit abroad. We are all of us potential autocrats, seekers for special privileges and social snobs. Against these characteristics, the gospel of Christ stands opposed.

There has always been agreement that the Master spoke to the heart and mind of the individual,—"After this manner pray ye." "Enter ye in at the strait gate." "Go and do thou likewise." "Follow me." So one might multiply injunctions from among his recorded words. However he also spoke much of the Kingdom and he established a fellowship of friends and disciples. The personal application of the gospel is not sufficient to safeguard human personality. We are born into families, are members of communities and citizens of a state. No one of us is able to live or to die to himself. Here is a family, let us say, on a farm in Europe in 1939. They are interested in their own concerns of daily living. What had they to do with the rise of Hitler and the struggle among nations? Yet all at once they are involved in catastrophe with no choice of their own. As society grows more complex the individual becomes less able to determine his own destiny. The solution of a Thoreau is not practicable. We cannot withdraw from the web even if it were possible or right to do so. Therefore the social application of the gospel is essential. The teaching of Christ must be applied not simply to individuals but to every social organism, to nations, to parties, to boards of directors, to labor unions, to the entire economic and social life of our civilization, in order that men may be enabled to live as the children of God, as personalities of infinite worth. The world must be made possible for Christians. As a matter of fact we cannot draw a simple line between the personal and the social or the physical and the spiritual. I learned the latter truth during the first world war when I discovered that it was extremely difficult to pray when suffering from the cold. The rebuilding of the economic life of devastated areas in the world goes hand in hand with the rekindling of spiritual fervor. It is not sufficient to give out tracts to those who are starving or cold or without opportunity. It was no accident that the Master chose that passage of great social significance when he read in the synagogue at Nazareth: "The Spirit of the Lord is upon me, because he hath anointed me to preach the gospel to the poor, . . . to heal the broken-hearted, to preach

88

deliverance to the captives, and recovery of sight to the blind, to set at liberty them that are bruised." All this as well as "to preach the acceptable year of the Lord." In the parable he counseled the clothing of the naked, the feeding of the hungry and the visiting of those in prison. In the protecting of human personality, the Church must reach into every field of human activity. Let no one think that this position of the worth of the individual will be easy to maintain. In Europe many suffered imprisonment and persecution for this reason. The same test may come elsewhere in this rapidly changing world at any time. We can be grateful that those of other faiths and of no acknowledged faith have also adhered firmly to this truth. Indeed many of these men and women have had greater vision and shown more willingness to sacrifice than the majority within the Christian Churches. Here again is evidence that God works His purpose in the whole of life—a fact which should keep Christians sufficiently humble.

The second principle of Jesus' teaching peculiarly significant today is that of universalism. St. Paul especially applied this truth in his relationship to the Gentiles. "God hath made of one blood all nations of men for to dwell on all the face of the earth." "There is neither Greek nor Jew, circumcision nor uncircumcision, Barbarian, Scythian, bond nor free:

but Christ is all, and in all." Here Christianity cuts straight across the prejudices, the racial and national pride of men. The evidence of this pride of race is world-wide, in the caste system in India, in the racial situation in the Far East, in the relationship of black, white and yellow within the confines of the United States. Christianity recognizes only the great human family of God. Thus the Church must oppose any theories of racial superiority, as well as any selfish nationalism which proclaims, "My country right or wrong, but my country." To the Christian only God's law and will are supreme. This does not mean that there is no place for a Christian nationalism. That we are to love our neighbor does not imply the destruction of individuality or of the family. The acid test of men and of institutions from the Christian point of view is found in the words: "He that is greatest among you shall be as one that serveth." The great nations of races of men in the eyes of God are not necessarily those with great economic or military powers but those who have the vision and the practice of the service of God and of man. Here is the test to gauge the value of every institution.

The Church in the proclamation of this universalism will find herself many times in opposition to the mind and the temper of the times. Ideas of racial and national superiority are difficult to destroy. In the right handling of the whole question of national sovereignty lies a key to the future peace and prosperity of mankind. The Church will boldly take her stand for worldwide brotherhood because of faith in God who is the Father of all.

The Church, however, cannot preach these truths sincerely and effectively without practicing them within her own fellowship. We constantly speak of the Church as the Body of Christ. The Master used his body even to the death on the Cross. The Church if she truly be the Body of Christ is to be so used in accomplishment of the will of God. If men see the Church protecting and anxious for her own possessions, her own life as an institution, tempering her judgments, message and action to meet current favor and support, then they will not be impressed by the preaching of the gospel of sacrifice. If the Church teaches the value of the individual and does not practice the principle in Church government, the teaching will seem shallow and insincere. If the Church does not in her own fellowship break down the inner walls of partition between races and nationalities, then she will have betrayed her Master. I realize full well that there are many practical difficulties and problems resulting from age-long differences and distinctions. But that was true in the days of the early Church. There is an absoluteness in the gospel, "Are ye able to drink of the cup that I shall drink of and to be baptized with the baptism that I am baptized with?" The early disciples might have compromised with the Roman State on the theory that education would accomplish results in the long run. But it was the very absoluteness of their stand which made a lasting impression upon the ancient world. Here, then, are issues which demand of the present disciples of Christ the same qualities of forthrightness and of courage. When people question as to the relevance of Christianity and of the Church to the pressing problems of the present, I think of Christ's teachings as to the eternal worth of human personality, of the universalism of his gospel and of his command to lose one's self in ministry to others. Could anything be more relevant to the immediate issues of today?

There have been those who have also questioned the practicality of the ethics of Jesus in a world of stern facts. We have been told by self-styled hard-headed men that it is impossible to apply his teaching to modern life. Well the method of these so-called realists has led us into a sadly disrupted world order. Is it not clear that the principles taught and lived by Jesus afford the only possible basis for world peace, for economic cooperation, for the well-being of every institution in our complex social system? To be sure he gave us an ideal. But the point is, it is a goal toward which we can and must work with the help of God. If life is only a bitter struggle for existence and has no more meaning than that, then the entire religious concept is untrue. But if, as the Christian believes, the world is God's creation and men are the children of God, then the true realist is the man who sees life from the point of view of the eternal and who tries sincerely to live according to the way of Christ. The Church has a true evangel for our day, magnificent and thrilling in vision and purpose. The Christian mission is not a visionary obsession of peculiar people but the very redemption of human life—a task which is the opportunity and the responsibility of every disciple of the Master. By the mission of the Church we mean the spread of the gospel throughout the world. Perhaps not since the days of St. Paul has the world been so conditioned for this effort. But the mission of the Church demands also that every aspect of our civilization be filled with the Spirit of God in Christ. The task is not only horizontal, it is vertical, as in the presence of God we see the self-centeredness, the sin of our civilization. The Church need not approach this task with apology or in a spirit of defeatism. All things are possible with God. The way of the Master is the truth.

The final resource of the Church I shall discuss is the presence and the guidance of the Holy Spirit. God is transcendent but we may be grateful that He is also immanent in the world He has created, in nature, in history and in the hearts and minds of those especially who respond to Him. The promise of the Master has been kept: "I will not leave you comfortless." One cannot penetrate the secret of the amazing power of the first Christian community without an appreciation of their intense conviction that they were constantly guided, strengthened and uplifted by the Spirit of God. This same experience has been present whenever the Church has been spiritually alive. True religion can never be second-hand; there must be a living, present experience.

This faith in the Holy Spirit means that life is not static or circumscribed, but that God's revelation of Himself is progressive. There was one of the great distinctions between the religion of the Master and that of the scribes. They reached their decisions by poring over the details of the Jewish law. But he in communion with God could declare, "I say unto you." He told his disciples, "Greater works than these shall he do." "Howbeit, when he, the Spirit of truth, is come he will guide you into all truth." In a pre vious chapter I have stressed the importance of the historical aspects of the Christian Church and of the gospel with especial emphasis upon the revelation of God in Christ. With the recognition of these factors, it is likewise true that Christians cannot always be looking back. In this there are great dangers of legalism and of a static traditionalism, which are certainly not characteristic of the life or the teaching of the Christ. In truth we have not begun to keep pace with him. He goes ahead as he did with his disciples. We shall need the strength and the guidance of the Holy Spirit to follow toward the goals he has set before us.

Of recent months science has been severely criticized due to the discovery of the new weapons of atomic warfare. However the spirit of true science has much to give us in the life of the Church. Professor Edmund W. Sinnott, Director of the Sheffield Scientific School in Yale University, delivered a lecture in 1944 on the subject, "Science and Education of Free Men." In this inspiring paper he discussed certain of the contributions of science: "Not least among these is a happy quality of all emancipated minds—the sense of adventure. Those ages when man's spirit has soared have always been times of launching out into the deep, of pushing beyond old horizons into the unknown. They have been eras of excitement over new lands, new ideas, when the vista of man's future widened and the world became a more expansive place. One fortunate quality of the spirit of science is that it helps to nourish this sense of adventure in a world too inclined to grow static and monotonous. This steady pushing out into the unknown, this never-ceasing conquest of new truth as years go by gives to the atmosphere of the laboratory a different quality from that which sometimes fills the chambers of the ivory tower. To men of science, truth is not a venerated body of doctrine, the great principles of which were long ago discovered by wiser men than we, who can only elaborate upon them. It is instead a growing, animated thing; warm as with life and often taking unexpected ways; not to be bound (however handsomely) in any hundred books but written rather in that great volume of the universe so many characters of which man yet must learn. It is this awareness of a vast body of truth still undiscovered but discoverable by those who have the skill to search for it which gives to science this spirit of adventure, this sense of great news to come." Religion emphasizes the initiative of God, whereas science stresses man's search for the truth. Both are essential. We are fellow laborers together with God. Religion can well pay heed to Dr. Sinnott's words as to the spirit of adventure.

The moment we make the Church and her teaching a closed book, confined solely to events of the past and held to an ecclesiastical narrow view of the truth, then we have missed the majesty, the breadth, the depth and the spiritual vitality of the life of the revelation of God in Christ—particularly the gift of the Holy Spirit who is to lead us into all truth. If this fact had been understood, how many unhappy controversies could have been avoided through the centuries. The Church instead of opposing would have welcomed the discoveries as to the nature of the universe and would not have tied up the old and untenable view with the faith of the Church. This mistake was made in regard to the theory of evolution. The battle which still continues surprisingly enough as to the interpretation of the Bible is another case in point. The understanding of the Bible due to the research of many scholars, far from undermining faith, gives an infinitely more inspiring and living record of God's dealing with men through progressive revelation than was possible under the theory that every word was of equal value because all were infallible. Furthermore the facts in the situation are beyond question to anyone with an open mind. The Christian reverences all truth as God's, no matter from whence this truth immediately comes. When Jesus commands his disciples to love God with all their mind, there is demanded integrity and courageous sincerity. No Christian should be fearful of facts. All types of fundamentalism, and there are many more than the Biblical variety, in essence are born of fear that some development may injure the faith. If the new factor is true, then no injury can come for truth is of God, whether the revelation come from the preacher, the poet or the worker in the laboratory. Infallibilities of ecclesiastical systems, of book or of opinion are mistaken doctrines born of timidity. In essence they reveal lack of faith in the presence and the guidance of the Spirit of God in all of life. We can be thankful for all that has been given us of the knowledge of God, but still we have so much to learn of Him; of His laws and of His ways. The Christian looks for continued revelation of His truth, with faith that God cannot contradict Himself. Any apparent conflicts are due to human misunderstanding and ignorance. Our response to God must not be moribund, static, legal but personal and vital—a great adventure based upon a living Faith in Him.

There is a balance which must be kept between the past, present and the future. On the one hand we must beware of the extreme represented by Tyrrell and Loisy who at their last stage would have largely ignored the historic characters of the gospel in favor of the theory of development. On the other hand we must not remain so bound by the past that we cannot meet, intelligently and courageously under God's guidance, the issues of today and tomorrow. The problem of Church Unity lies beyond the purpose and the scope of this book, but that question is an illustration of this very point. The Christian must be loyal to Christ. On this point all are agreed. On this basis the Roman Catholic cannot compromise the issue of the Papacy, or many Anglicans that of apostolic succession, or the Baptist the unquestioned method of Baptism in the New Testament, or the Congregationalist the principles of freedom. It does not seem possible that these differences can be resolved as a result of the research of scholars in the field of the New Testament and the Apostolic Age. After all the study the positions are maintained as before. The answer can only be found in an overpowering experience of the Holy Spirit. As a result there would be penitence for prejudice and the creation of a will to make the Church indeed the Body of Christ. In this as in other matters the difficulty is that we dare not trust ourselves to the guidance of God. As a matter of fact there is excellent historical precedent. The differences between the disciples of St. Paul and St. Peter were not small. The Jewish law had come as a covenant with God from the long and sacred past. To break with that tradition was a daring adventure. Yet there can be no question that the victory of the Pauline group made possible the future life of the Church. That decision made the difference between a Jewish sect and the Christian Church. Dean George Hodges liked to quote the text, "It seemed good to the Holy Ghost and to us." We must approach our problems today in the conviction that God lives, that He could if He so willed raise up of these stones children unto Abraham. Our task is to give ourselves so completely to Him that we may be able to witness with power in the world of today and tomorrow. Again the Church need not give way to fears and anxieties, for we have the comfort and the strength of the Holy Spirit.

Troeltsch distinguishes between three types of the sociological development of Christian thought, the Church, the sect and mysticism. "The Church," he writes, "is an institution which has been endowed with grace and salvation as the result of the work of Redemption, it is able to receive the masses, and to adjust itself to the world, because to a certain extent it can afford to ignore the need for subjective holiness for the sake of the objective treasures of grace and redemption." [3] The sect is a voluntary

[3] *Ibid.*, Vol. II, p. 993.

society composed of strict and definite believers bound to each other by the fact that all have experienced the "new birth." These believers live apart from the world, are limited to small groups. Mysticism means that the world of ideas which had hardened into formal worship and doctrine is transformed into a purely personal basis. Certainly any formal division of this kind can only be accepted in a general way. As Troeltsch himself declares, "From the beginning these three forms were foreshadowed, and all down the centuries to the present day wherever religion is dominant, they still appear alongside of one another while among themselves they are strangely and variously interwoven and interconnected." [4] In the controversies between Church and sect during the centuries the latter term has often been used as a term of reproach but it is in no such sense that I use this description at this time.

As we face the very great tasks ahead we shall need certain of the characteristics of these three groups. From what I have already said it must be clear that I believe in the Church, not only as a present company of faithful people but as a historic fellowship reaching back through the vicissitudes and the changes of the years to the time of the Master

[4] *Ibid.*, pp. 993-94.

himself and to which was given the responsibility
for carrying on his ministry of reconciliation. Because in the beginning of movements there is necessarily greater simplicity, we see most clearly in
the apostolic age, the clear-cut characteristics of this
community of faith and of life. As the gospel spread
and particularly as the Church was recognized offi-
cially by the State, the situation became complex.
The pressures resulting from persecution are powerful and direct. Much more subtle were the pressures
exerted in the time of acceptance and of popularity.
The Church could not possibly have survived as a
spiritual force unless there had been a body of faith,
or practice, or organization. How much of this was
directly due to the command of Christ, or how
much developed under the guidance of the Holy
Spirit in meeting exigencies which arose, will remain
a matter of belief rather than of proven historical
fact. It was essential that there be this development
to maintain continuity with the past, to insure a
certain definiteness and objectivity and to stress the
essential unity and universality of the fellowship.
During these many centuries many mistakes have
been made due to human frailty and sin. The wonder
is that, considering the attacks from without and the
weakness within, the Church has survived. But more
than counterbalancing these failures, there is the

story of wisdom, courage, faith and sacrifice. The Church has brought God in Christ to millions of men and women. We owe to this historic Church all the blessings which Christianity has given to us so abundantly. As we meet the manifold difficulties of our time, we shall be wise to consider the way by which the Church has lived. The general temper of our generation has been set against organized religion. But perhaps in the crucible of this hour we can better realize that personal or parochial effort, however essential, is not enough. Despite the present divisions of the Christian Church, there is much greater unity than is generally recognized. Faith in God, in the revelation of Christ, in the Bible as the Word of God, in the missionary cause, in prayer and sacrament, in life everlasting—these are infinitely more important in a battle against materialism than the matters about which we differ. These latter seem at present to center largely about the validity of various ministries. The faith of the Church is more important than the means by which that faith is expressed. In reality in a divided Christendom every so-called Church is a sect, for no communion has, whatever may be claimed, the whole truth of God. On the other hand every communion has revealed the fruits of the Spirit in devotion to God's will. What is needed on the part of every communion is a greater humility of spirit, a deepening of faith, a realization of the urgency of the times, and a surrender to the leading of God. With this there must be the willingness to share with others whatever blessings God has given. The Church cannot be regarded as a private club. It does not seem necessary to protect God or the truth, beyond the necessities of decent and reverent administration. The more all who call themselves Christians can have a common experience of God in Christ, the nearer will come the day when the Church Universal will become more than an ideal, a present spiritual reality.

The Churches must have as well something of the spirit and the intensity characteristic of the sect. If we compare some of the sects today with the larger Christian Communions, we may well be astonished by the greater sacrifice of the members of the sects in terms of money given, missionary zeal and downright convictions. The line between fanaticism and conviction is not always easy to draw. The early Christians were fanatics to the cultured Roman citizen. We may be certain that the world will not be won to Christ by a timid, cautious presentation of Christianity. There must be conviction, daring and willingness to sacrifice. Those who belong to the sects have always thought of themselves as set

against the world. As a small boy I was well acquainted with two Shaker communities. There they
always spoke of those outside the Shaker fold as
"world's people." The ideal of the Church includes
all mankind. But particularly in abnormal times, such
as these, the Church must be set against much that
is in the world. In a very real sense true Christians
in every age have been a peculiar people. No one
dare predict the future. It is reasonable to envisage
at least the possibility of a time when the Church
could be driven once again to the catacombs.
Whether this eventuates or not, the Churches can
well develop certain of the characteristics of the
sect.

Finally the Church cannot lose the experience of
the mystic. There is too much truth in Walter Lippmann's description of the organized Churches:
"Fundamentally the great Churches are secular institutions; they are governments preoccupied inevitably with the regulations of the unregenerate
appetites of mankind. In their scriptures there is to
be found the teaching that true salvation depends
upon internal reform of desire. But since this reform
is so very difficult, in practice the Churches have
devoted themselves not so much to making real
conversions, as to governing the dispositions of the

unconverted multitude." [5] It is essential that the Church keep the first-hand deep personal experience of God in Christ. There is never any apology needed for the life of the seer and the saint. The organization of the visible Church is necessary, else the Church would be, as has been said, "A soul without a body" and we must have bodies in this world. But the Church must not be a body without a soul. All the organization would be as sounding brass and tinkling cymbal unless men are lead to know God, to live in companionship with Christ, to experience here and now eternal life. Prayer, self-discipline, communion with God—these are the very life blood of the Church. However important history may be, every true Christian must know God, however imperfectly, for himself. That is as true of the laity as of the clergy. Christianity is infinitely more than a moral code, it is a living fellowship based upon a deep personal as well as common conviction and experience.

The Christian Church has great resources from the past and in the present, a noble tradition of the heroes and saints of all the centuries and a living faith strengthening and guiding men in meeting the necessities of today. Like Elisha's young companion,

[5] *Preface to Morals*, p. 201, Macmillan. Copyright 1929 by Walter Lippmann. Used by permission.

we may take comfort in the words of the prophet, "Fear not; for they that be with us are more than they that be with them." Or as St. Paul described a similar experience, "If God be for us, who can be against us?"

# V

## A LESSON FROM HISTORY

OUR GENERATION is caught in the vortex of rapidly moving and tragic events. The danger is that as a result we suffer from hysteria, which in turn will cause us to lose judgment and a proper sense of proportion. Already there are evidences both to the right and to the left that this is the case. Under the compulsions of the hour we are generating more heat than light. We must somehow find it possible to gain greater objectivity and perspective. One way of doing this is to turn to the past not as a means of escape from the problems of the present, but in order that we may face these conditions with new understanding, with more wisdom and patience. Men who cannot discuss dispassionately the modern questions of Russia, of socialism, of labor and capital, of free enterprise and governmental control, can read of the perplexities and innovations of ancient Greece or Rome without a noticeable rise in blood pressure. Especially for Christians who are fearful

for the faith and for the Church, it is well for us
to remind ourselves that both have survived many
cataclysms in the past two thousand years. When we
feel that no age has been forced to face such difficulties as ours, it is a cure for self-pity to turn to
history and to read again of strong men who by faith
subdued kingdoms and wrought righteousness. History never repeats itself exactly. As Christians we
repudiate the pagan idea of meaningless cycles. It is
never desirable or possible to recreate the past. However there are striking parallels, and there are lessons
to be learned from the school of experience. Many
ideas which currently pass as modern are to be found
in the popular notions of antiquity. What I propose
to do is to take a period of political and spiritual
collapse into which was born a new and vital power
to see if in such a period we can find some light and
leading for today. I have in mind the years which
marked the disintegration of the Roman Empire—
for nowhere else in recorded history can we find
greater similarities to our world of the present. There
are many obvious differences. The geographical extent of the ancient world was limited but on the
other hand the whole of existing civilization was
involved. The period of the decline and the fall
extended over several centuries, a discouraging
thought to contemplate. But with the increased

tempo of life it is very likely that processes which once took centuries, may now work themselves out in much less time.

Charles Norris Cochrane has written a book entitled *Christianity and Classical Culture,* which seems to me peculiarly helpful and penetrating. For much that immediately follows I am indebted to this thoroughly documented and yet broad-visioned study of both antiquity and Christianity in the first four centuries.

There have been many reasons given for the fall of the Roman Empire. Some have held that it was death from old age, others that empires by necessity expand until they burst. Still others have sought the answer in the field of economics and outside pressure upon the Empire. The most obvious diagnosis has been to point to the rise of the power of the barbarian multitudes. Then there has been mentioned disease and the exhaustion of natural resources. Within the Empire the debilitating effect of constant warfare, rampant social evils such as slavery, and the political failure to solve the problem of the succession all played their part. Mr. Cochrane then goes on to give his own estimate of the underlying causes which led to disintegration. "The debacle, however, was not merely economic or social or political, or rather it was all of these because it was something more. For what here confronts us is in the last analysis a moral and intellectual failure, a failure of the Graeco-Roman mind. From this standpoint we are not concerned to enter into a dispute as to the relative importance of the various theories proposed but may freely admit that they all have a place within the complex tissue of material fact. If, however, the Romans themselves proved unable to come to grips with that fact, the reason must surely be supposed to lie in some radical defect of their thinking. In this defect we may find the ultimate explanation of the nemesis which was operating to bring about the decline and fall of ancient civilizations. The doom which awaited Romanitas was that of a civilization which failed to understand itself and was in consequence dominated by a haunting fear of the unknown." [1] The deepest failure was, therefore, that of classical culture which, while it underwent various revivals as in the time of Augustus and much later of Julian, was never able to meet the spiritual and the intellectual needs of men.

It is impossible here to pursue further Mr. Cochrane's discussion of classical thought in many writers of antiquity. Classicism had two dominant characteristics, one a belief in virtue, character—"strictly human excellence by powers strictly human," a mat-

[1] P. 157, Oxford University Press. Used by permission.

111

ter of form, of adhering to the type—exemplified by the terms art and industry. The second characteristic was an emphasis upon the necessity of fortune, "good luck." "The power deemed necessary to protect civilization, was supposed to depend upon a fortunate coincidence of character and of circumstances, a coincidence thought to have been finally realized in the person of Augustus." [2] In line with these two emphases an adherent of the classical tradition was on the one hand asked to lift himself by his own boot straps. With the admonition to think of himself as a mere man, he was nevertheless expected to overcome the circumstances of life by the force of his own character, fortified by heroic examples from the past. On the other hand finding this an impossible task by himself he is regarded as subject to the chances of fate. If he is to have bad luck then nothing he can be or do by himself will have any effect. To achieve success there must be that combination of character and of fortune. The result was that men found themselves bound by the hands of fate. They were led to all kinds of excesses in order to find some method of escape. Many Romans became prey to various types of pagan mysticism. Of course there was in classicism much that was noble. Lucretius for example realized the

[2] *Ibid.*, p. 160.

danger of faith in the traditional gods of paganism, resulting in absurd efforts to win their favor and support. His answer was to rule out the gods entirely. As Mr. Cochrane states, "His philosophy offers to mankind emancipation from the terrors of the unseen and the impalpable: and to replace the vast aspirations of pagan mysticism, it proposes a goal of life, because it is independent of support from superhuman powers, is not doomed in advance to frustration. What Lucretius thus advocates is in a word salvation by enlightenment." [3] But whether with or without the gods the believer in classicism was doomed to frustration. His faith in the line of emperors as supermen was shattered by the reality of events. As the forces of the Empire weakened he became disillusioned as to the eternal character of the imperial regime. It was not only that there were the pressures from without to be met, within were no resilient forces of the Spirit. Fortitude, resignation, the seeking of omens were not enough as the Empire disintegrated. The idols of classicism became shattered by the pressure of the times. This recalls the statement of Toynbee that civilizations die not because of pressures from without but from suicide within. The Roman might cry with anguish, Who shall deliver us from the body of this death? To the

[3] *Ibid.*, p. 36.

majority there was no answer but disillusionment and despair.

Into such a world came the gospel of Christ and of the Christian Church. Again there is not time here to trace Mr. Cochrane's study of the development of Christian thought by the post-Nicene Fathers, especially Augustine. But his conclusion is that in this formulation and the expression of the Christian faith there came new power into the minds and hearts of men, which, unable to prevent the destruction of the ancient civilization, did nevertheless prepare the way "for a new and radically different future." At no time was the result as simple as this. There were retreats and advances. The temporal victory of Christianity was both a help and a hindrance. As Mr. Cochrane wrote of the Church in one period, "To envisage the faith as a political principle was not so much to Christianize civilization as to civilize Christianity, it was not to consecrate human institutions to the service of God but rather to identify God with the maintenance of human institutions. While therefore, under governmental pressure the empire rapidly shed the trappings of secularism to assume those of Christianity, it remained at heart profoundly pagan." [4] The answer was to be found not in the externals of government and of life, but

[4] *Ibid.*, p. 336.

114

in the deep experience of God in Christ with the complete dedication of the mind to God in the formulation of Christian doctrine. Instead of man being mere man he was the child of God. Instead of feeling bound by the necessities of nature, there was faith in a God, Creator of Heaven and Earth, who so loved that He gave. Instead of a sense of being buffeted by ill fortune and having to seek good luck, men knew themselves the servants of a God whose service is perfect freedom. Faith instead of being static and an idealization of the past became living and vital. Instead of a society based upon the struggle for power, the Christian community was a fellowship based "upon the power of love." Through the Christian Church came new hope and strength to the individual, and through those inspired men and women to a disintegrating world. That there were distortions in their teaching of the Church no one can deny. But many of these were unquestionably due to the character and the exigencies of the times. It is unfair to judge any man apart from consideration of the generation in which he lived. But when these peculiarities have been admitted, it must be stated that Christian theologians performed a magnificent service. In the midst of the dying civilization of classicism they had the knowledge, the insight and the daring to use the partial truths found in

Greek philosophy and to adapt these tools to the formulation and the expression of Christianity. The formulation of truth is not all that was necessary. Combined with this there were Christian experience and Christian living. Dr. T. R. Glover has stated that the early Church out-thought, out-lived and out-died the pagan world. To quote Mr. Cochrane again, speaking of the Christian struggle, he wrote: "What it demands is a united effort of hand and heart and head in order to expose the fictitious character of secular valuations and to vindicate the reality of Christian claims." [5] This is what with all the admitted limitations, the Church was able to do through the period of the decline and the fall of the Roman Empire. It is this continuing battle against secularism and paganism which the Church is called upon to wage today. Indeed the point of view of classicism is not different from that held by many of the intelligentsia of the modern world. "Salvation through enlightenment" has a familiar sound as does the emphasis upon men's potentialities apart from any relationship to God. Many a modern could be pictured in terms of Mr. Cockrane's description of Tacitus: "With him what replaces faith is a lively interest in human beings which combines vague aspirations for personal immortality with a sense that

[5] *Ibid.*, p. 516.

men really survive in the memory of posterity." [6]
If on the one hand many of the so-called intellectuals today reveal many points of view held by the philosophers and teachers of antiquity, on the other hand the ancient theory of the necessity of good luck has great popular adherence. We pride ourselves upon our scientific outlook and our freedom from superstition but the fact is that superstition is widely rampant. We should be surprised, I imagine, if we actually knew the number influenced in daily decisions by a belief in astrology, to say nothing of fortune tellers, mediums and other evidences of a false supernaturalism. The people who knock on wood, refuse to sit down thirteen at a table, and have various curious ways of escaping ills or of propitiating good fortune are simply a matter of daily observation. We return to the proposition that the difficulty in our confused and tragic world is not simply political or economic but mental and spiritual. The diagnosis of the ancient world is decidedly apropos: "For what here confronts us is in the last analysis a moral and intellectual failure. The doom which awaited Romanitas was that of a civilization which failed to understand itself and was in consequence dominated by a haunting fear of the

[6] *Ibid.*, p. 136.

unknown." [7] It is imperative that we face the fact that such a sentence hangs over us today. There is confusion in the political and economic fields but the greatest danger rests in the fact that due to many causes we have failed to understand ourselves in relation to the will and purpose of the everlasting God, from whence have we come? What is the meaning of our transitory lives? What is the goal toward which we are moving as individuals and as a society? These are questions which cannot be answered by the headlines in the daily press nor by the fluctuations in contemporary events. They can only be met by the determined effort of mind and of heart.

We need to realize for one thing that ideas are important. We have seen how the thought of theologians profoundly influenced the course of events. Professor F. S. C. Northrop's book, *The Meeting of East and West,* makes the same point. Millions of people who never heard of John Locke have had their lives affected by his philosophy in many of the patterns of our democracy. An even more dramatic illustration is the present result and turmoil due to the thinking of Karl Marx. LeCompte du Noüy writes, "No one can deny the fact that mankind is governed by forces derived from ideas. The outcome

[7] *Ibid.,* p. 157.

of certain abstract ideas transformed our material environment (applied science, machines) and shaped our private and social life but the incentive and inspiration of man is to be found in what might be termed 'lever ideas'—superstitions, ambitions and religious ideas. Any theory which neglects them and takes into consideration only the physical welfare of mankind, considered as a flock, is incomplete and inadequate." [8] Professor Alfred N. Whitehead devotes an entire book to the subject *Adventures of Ideas*. He writes, "A general idea is always a danger to the existing order. The whole bundle of its conceivable special embodiment in various usages of society constitutes a program of reform. At any moment the smouldering unhappiness of mankind may seize on some such program and initiate a rapid change guided by the light of its doctrines. In this way the conception of the dignity of human nature was quietly energizing in the minds of Roman officials. For six hundred years the ideal of the intellectual and moral grandeur of the human soul had haunted the ancient Mediterranean world. . . . It was the faint light of the dawn of a new order of life. In the midst of this period of progress and decadence Christianity arose. The progress of humanity can be defined as the process of transforming society so as to make the

[8] *Human Destiny*, p. 124, Longmans.

original Christian ideals increasingly practicable for its individual members." [9]

This emphasis upon the importance of ideas runs counter to the popular present notion that so-called practical action is all that really counts. The newspaper headlines are seized by the politicians, by the generals, by the organizers of industry and of labor. An exception may be found of the individual who makes possible some startling advance in the fields of science or of health. But as history has shown again and again, there may be some thinker in some quiet place, unknown by his fellows, who by virtue of an idea may make an even more important contribution to the public good.

The Churches have been greatly influenced by this cult of action. On the whole, even within many Churches, there is little interest in the study of ideas. We are long on programs, campaigns and slogans. Obviously these are important and have their place. But we are finding now the weakness resulting from ignoring the deeper aspects of the Christian life. We can do this only at our peril. It is not enough to be on our way. We must know where we are going. Behind our activity there must be the result of the labors of scholars and of thinkers. It is my conviction that the theologian must play an increasingly vital

[9] Pp. 17-18, Macmillan. Copyright 1933. Used by permission.

rôle in the world of today and tomorrow. I mean much more by this than the teaching of systematic theology to generations of theological students, important as that is. I mean creative thinking based upon the discipline of knowledge, of study and of prayer and worship which will help this age to escape the sentence of death placed upon Roman civilization through the failure of the mind to grasp the deeper spiritual and moral truths. Those of us who are engaged necessarily in the ministry of action must rely upon the theologian, and I use that term in no technical narrow sense but to include broadly all those who in many fields of scholarship are seeking to know and to apply the will and purpose of God. These are the key people of our time and their number must be increased. This point of view may seem strange coming from one whose ministry has been spent in pastoral and administrative tasks. Years ago when I returned from a chaplaincy in the first world war, I was asked to become an instructor in the Episcopal Seminary at Cambridge. In talking this over with Dr. Edward S. Drown, the Professor of Theology, I said, "But I could not do this even if I had the ability. I must be out among people, men, women, boys and girls, of every walk of life." I have always remembered his reply given with deep emotion, "God forbid that anyone should ever teach in a seminary who has not paid the price of that sacrifice." Now I should like to turn that about. Those of us engaged in the ministry of action pay an equal price in the sacrifice of the opportunity to study steadfastly and continuously without great interruption and to have the time to think without the pressure of immediate duty. It is a weakness that today the faculties of most of our seminaries are so understaffed that there are indeed few who can escape these pressures. But the world, all of us, today, need the result of the knowledge and the insight of the scholar who is a man of God. Let me give some illustrations of this need.

It is a commonplace to state the fact of the tremendous progress made by science in the past fifty years. But too often all that is popularly meant by this is reference to the invention of machines or tools which increase our production, our speed or our comfort. These are by no means negligible in effect upon our lives. But science reaches out into more distant and more significant areas, invisible worlds of force and of power, of which the atomic bomb is the most important and awesome result. The world, the universe, assume a new aspect. The assumptions of an earlier static cut-and-dried science have already become outmoded. A revolution has taken place as radical as the Copernican theory in another day. Still we are on the verge apparently of even more important and striking discoveries in many fields of science. These new truths need interpretation by the Christian thinker. Of course it is possible to say that all this has no bearing upon the problems of faith,—that religion, and science, fundamentally relate themselves to different fields. This opinion has been strengthened in the past by the unwise and unhappy battle waged at times by the Church against scientific truth. But while it is true that science and religion do deal with different aspects of truth, nevertheless every discovery is related to the truth of God. The Psalmist wrote, "The heavens declare the glory of God; and the firmament showeth his handiwork." This statement is as true today as it was then. What have these new truths taught us as to the nature and being of God the Creator? The question is deeper than the resolving of an imaginary, even an actual, conflict between religion and science. It has to do with a modern revelation of the power and character of the eternal God. The greatness of the writers of the first chapter of Genesis was that they took the simple science of their day and said, "In the beginning God." It is just this which is needed today. For so many, who by no stretch of the imagination could be called scientists, have made popular science their God. True science needs interpretation in the light of the affirmation of a reasonable faith. "In the beginning God." The difficulty is that as generally only Republicans and Democrats attend their own party rallies, so the scientist works in his own field and the theologian in his and never the twain do meet. It is hopeful that there are many eminent scientists who understand the significance and the necessity of the spiritual. These are making an increasing contribution to the struggle against the secularism of our time—because of their position in the realm of special knowledge. But we need theologians who can also bridge this gap, who by study understand the intricacies of scientific truth and can interpret this truth in the light of the eternal truth of God. As an illustration let me take the comparatively recent development of psychiatry. The field of human personality has always been and is today a mysterious one. The psychiatrist has achieved astonishing results in many cases with the shock treatment, yet he does not know why this is true, what happens as a result within the human organism. Beyond question the psychiatry of the present, with all the progress made, is primitive with what will be known and practiced in coming decades. The public already expects too much of this new science, which is not a substitute for but an auxiliary to religion and the invisible forces of human strength and character. But the fact is that through the psychiatrist we have had opened to us new vistas into human nature, new revelations of God's truth. These revelations are supremely important for the pastor and the teacher, in the cure of human souls and in the wise guidance of men. But they are also important in the understanding of men as the children of the Creator and as a manifestation of the character of the eternal God. The field is so complex that it is not enough to have a few clergymen on the side interested in this subject. There should be those in the Christian Church, both clergy and laity, who are devoting themselves completely to this subject, that, from the Christian point of view, we may know the implications and may take advantage in the broadest possible way of the results. A cleavage which already partially exists between this new science and the Christian faith would indeed be disastrous and also unnecessary. There are many Christian psychiatrists who realize profoundly the significance of the Christian religion to this field. Increasingly the Church is aware of these developments. The need is for the study of this area by competent students, that all this truth may be put to the service of God and of man.

In the same way the contemporary world should be held under constant survey. The prophets saw in history the working of the hand of God. The moves of Egypt, of Persia, of Assyria, as well as those of the leaders of the Kingdoms of Israel and Judah were studied with discrimination and interpreted in the light of the judgment of God. Today economists, internationalists, military and political leaders study constantly the shifting scenes of world events. But this is also the field of the Christian counterpart of the prophet of old. Prejudice cannot rule our decisions certainly. Sentiment is a questionable guide. There must be a knowledge of the facts. Then there must be the ability to face these facts in the light of eternity. Certainly the prophet of old would see the international scene in broader terms than can the statesmen, who must wrestle with more immediate solutions and problems. But amid the uncertainty and the fear of today we need the message of an Isaiah, "In quietness and confidence shall be your strength." Above the clamor of the peace conferences, of the struggles of nations and of ideologies, there must come to us the dispassionate interpretation as far as this is possible, while we see through a glass darkly, of the Will of God. This can come only from men of wisdom who have at the same time knowledge of the world and an experience of the living God.

So one might continue with many more illustrations of this vitally important task before the Church, in general so superbly accomplished by the early

Church, namely the facing of the world in every field of life and of activity with Christian truth. There are those who would advocate that in so doing it is necessary to scrap all the experience and knowledge of preceding generations. We have had calls for "a new theology" with patronizing estimates of Christian interpretations of other days. If you have followed me thus far, you will realize how shallow such a demand is. There are, we are confident, new revelations of the truth of God but we can only appreciate and rightly appraise these as they are kept in focus with the experience of other generations. I venture to say that there can be no deep exposition of Christian truth today which does not take into careful and informed account all that has gone on before. We must have a deeper knowledge of the past to be able to withstand the storms of the present.

What I am trying to say is that we must mobilize the intellectual power of Christian men and women. The Church has beyond question lost much ground in intellectual circles. It is easy to dismiss this fact by blaming indifference, or materialism for this result. The Church has also been at fault. We have not been loving God with our minds. The consequence is that men who respect the processes of human reasoning have been drawn into other fields of study and of research, into science, or economics or to law.

This fact has conditioned the attitude of the great mass of people. Ideas do have in the long run a profound popular effect. As Evelyn Underhill has written, "Without its metaphysical background religion easily declines into a mere system of sanctions and consolations. You must or you mustn't do this. Be good and you will be happy." We have been content to be Christian exhorters or program makers, but the essential task is to be a Christian teacher, if we are to lead our civilization from the judgment which fell upon Rome.

I do not wish to be misunderstood. It is, of course, the pure in heart who see God. Many times those who are childlike in faith experience God in a deeper sense than do the wise and prudent. No intellectual approach to God can give the deepest answers. The saints have been by no means the best informed, but their spiritual quality has given them an exceptional effectiveness akin to wisdom. The Church is fortunately made up of all kinds and conditions of men and women, and there is a place and an opportunity for each and every one. All I am saying is not depreciating the religion of the heart, for true religion is a personal relationship best described by the analogy of a son and his father and a man and his brother. But it is true that God has given men their minds which are equally with the heart to be consecrated to Him. Inadequate to the majesty of God are all formulations which attempt to explain Him, but nevertheless we cannot do without these formulations and without the consecration of mind which compels us to these efforts. Faith is more than reason but faith cannot be unreasonable. Who can adequately estimate the contribution of Christian thinkers from St. Paul to the present day?

People are filled with questions and also a deep yearning for some certainty, for a power, a Person greater than they are. They are confused and ignorant. Popular science caught their imagination and now they realize vaguely that science may destroy rather than perpetuate civilization. They have had their faith in an infallible Bible destroyed and yet they have not by-and-large been taught, so that they could understand, the constructive aspect of the new interpretation of the Bible. They have developed a pride in human accomplishment, only to see man destroy his fellow in recurring wars, accompanied by evidences of complete human degradation, and thus many have lost faith in humanity and in themselves. Everywhere the picture is the same—men, confused, ignorant, and yet longing for greater vision and knowledge and strength. The cry is again that of the ancient world, "Who shall deliver us from the body of this death?" The Church has not seemed important in a world of scientific and of social revolution, and has only been tolerated and patronized because the trumpet of faith has given forth no certain sound. Without faith and conviction there has been no heroic and sacrificial living on a basis which could influence the course of events. The Churches have been too greatly interested in secondary matters. Now we are compelled by the very pressure of events to come to grips with realities in the world in which we live and with the nature, purpose and will of the eternal God. What of God and the new weapons of destruction? What of God and the desperate plight of million upon million of our brethren? What of God and nationalism? What of God and democracy and communism? What of God and science, of God and history? These and many more issues press upon us and must be met by study, by thought, by prayer and by determined and sacrificial action. Nothing in our world can be considered as alien to the Christian gospel and to the Christian Church for all of life belongs to God. Men are anxiously awaiting an answer to these and many more questions like them. For upon the answers hang issues of life and of death. The answers must be something infinitely more than the repetition of traditional phrases out of the past or shallow catch-words from the present. I believe that these answers must be more than the voice of unquestioned authority though there are always those who will find at least temporary peace in being relieved of the necessity of thinking. These answers must come from the mind, the heart, the experience of a Christian fellowship devoted to the will of God and to discipleship of a Master who gave of himself to the death on the Cross. There can be nothing so vital as this task. Whether the Churches in their entire membership respond to the needs of the hour may well be open to question. But certainly there must be many consecrated men and women within the fellowship of the Churches who will rise to the opportunity and the responsibility. I turn again to the quotation from Professor Whitehead: "A general idea is always a danger to the existing order. The whole bundle of its conceivable special embodiment in various usages constitutes a program of reform. At any moment the smouldering unhappiness of mankind may seize upon some such program and initiate a rapid change guided by the light of its doctrines." [10] Certainly in these days, there is abundant evidence of the unhappiness of mankind, never more so in all human history to such a widespread extent. Yet in the light of this fact the same old remedies are being attempted—balance of power, national self-interest, preparation for war. If we know anything we must

[10] *Op. cit.*, p. 17.

know that here are no far-reaching solutions for the manifold ills of mankind. At best they are only temporary palliatives to tide matters over until the next crisis arises. Yet here are the great ideas of the living God, Father of all men of every nation and race, of the Christ who is the Way and the Truth, of a guiding Spirit who draws men into deep fellowship one with another in a life governed by the love of the brethren and the promise of the life of the world to come. These I have spoken of as ideas but in many, many cases they have been and are so much more— convictions and experiences as deep and as personal as are any which come to the minds and the hearts of men. If only the uncertainty and the groping of the present hour could give way to the certainty of God's Will and of the way of the Master. If only these great ideas—of worship, of unselfish service, of brotherhood could be a danger to the existing order! Such has been the case in the past. Never has Christian truth or Christian living won a final or complete victory. But there have been times when Christianity has profoundly influenced the course of human events, when great spiritual ideals have resulted in effective action. Here again there may be such a period. Many of the necessary ingredients are present—a profound disillusionment with the ways of a civilization which has produced war after war with all the catastrophic results in human suffering and loss, an eager longing on the part of untold millions for a better way. Here again is a period when the scales seem to hang in the balance. A Church consecrated in mind and heart, deeply convinced, and of heroic action can once again be the light of the world in a time of darkness. This calls, we must continue to remind ourselves, for infinitely more than the complacency, the mere outward respectability and conventionality, the softness and the shallowness of all too much of contemporary Church life. The times demand a dynamic effort of mind, of heart and of will through the power of the Spirit of God. This effort calls for the cooperation of every member of the Christian Church. I have stressed the intellectual needs of the day and I believe that these are essential in the struggle else Christianity will lose a strength and a substance, and become simply emotion. We must mobilize in the name of Christ scholars, teachers and scientists. But also we must have men and women of heart, will and action who by what they believe and have experienced will be in themselves witnesses to Christ in every walk of life. This is a task beyond the ability of the clergy of the Church alone. One of the weaknesses of contemporary Church life is that so little is asked spiritually of lay men and women. It is necessary to emphasize that this is a task for everyone in his own vocation and ministry.

We may be certain that the Church, either large or small, above the ground or underground, will continue to live. The past proves this beyond dispute. The real question is, in these crucial times, will the Church of Christ rise to the greatness of the opportunity and responsibility? In a period of decline and of fall, we have seen that the Church performed a magnificent service for God and man. With the help of God, this can happen here.

# VI

## *THE MINISTER*

THE OPPORTUNITIES and responsibilities which confront the Christian minister remain essentially the same from generation to generation. At present, however, due to the urgency of the times these are accentuated. Comparison is often made between the position of the parson when he was in a unique sense the person of the community and today when he stands in the eyes of many only on the periphery of momentous events and when in a sense he has many competitors in the field of public service, in the newspaper, on the air, and in the offices of the psychiatrists among others. Such a contrast is hardly true to the facts. It is simply the emphasis which has changed. There was a time when the clergyman by virtue of his ordination and official position stood almost *ex officio* in a position of leadership. In general, with the secularization of life and in the complexity of our social system, this has ceased to be true. Nevertheless a clergyman of conviction, of wisdom, and possessed of qualities of leadership, can still exert a profound influence upon his community. For still speaking to the deepest needs of mankind, he is the exponent of the eternal gospel. The change of emphasis lies in the fact that nothing is assumed or taken for granted. The acid test is applied, "By their fruits they shall be known." The modern clergyman must stand on his own feet for what he is rather than for what he is presumed to be. If this has certain obvious disadvantages, there are also benefits. There is a reality and an exigency which demand the very best in his life. The minister must be able to face the facts courageously, with no special privilege of position or of sentiment, even as the Master met his generation, for we must recall that he held no position and even at times had no place to lay his head. All of this calls for quality in the minister of today with extraordinary gifts of faith and of wisdom.

The primary task of the clergyman as of the Church is to testify to the living God. This should be true of men in every walk of life but it is the special vocation of the clergyman. He is in the ministry, we trust, because he has been called by God. This does not mean that he has had a vision like those described in the Bible as vouchsafed to the prophets and apostles. Indeed the call may be more convincing because it has come through judgments, continued prayer for guidance, the advice of family and friends and sometimes the pressure of events. It is comforting to many to realize that Phillips Brooks attempted to be a school teacher and failed tragically. Dr. A. V. G. Allen, his biographer, writes of this period, "The six months which elapsed after his leaving the Latin School are seen in the light of these letters to his friend to have been a dreary and gloomy period when the depression of his spirit reached the lowest degree." [1] After reaching the seminary, he wrote in a letter, "Consider myself here without debating how I got here." Can anyone doubt in the light of his future ministry that he was called by God to his vocation? It was necessary that the door to teaching be shut in his face. So God leads us in many ways until there comes a certainty that the ministry is the will of God. Without that conviction no sincere and humble-minded man would dare to proceed to ordination. His theological education should mean a strengthening of his purpose. There have been and are seminaries so narrow that they have seemed to constrict the truth of God. But the seminary at the best affords an opportunity which rarely comes again of a community of like-minded faculty and student body living in a fellowship of worship and of work.

[1] *Life and Letters of Phillips Brooks,* Vol. I, p. 122, Dutton.

Later on the minister faces many interruptions and difficult decisions as to the use of his time, but in the seminary ideally he has the privilege of wide and constant reading and study. To many, after the decision has been made, the years of seminary life particularly in prospect seem to be an unnecessary burden. But in view of the exacting tasks ahead these years are invaluable and it cannot be too strongly stated that short cuts are inadvisable. The prospective minister who tries to save time by neglecting seminary training is similar to a woodsman who has so much to do that he has no time to sharpen his axe. In the seminary too there is the understandable urge to be at the actual practical tasks of the ministry as soon as possible. The alumni of most seminaries are always complaining that recent graduates are not taught the essential routines of the ministry. My opinion about this is that if the choice must be made, the practicalities of how to conduct a parish canvass or to hold a baby in baptism and a thousand other useful details can be learned in the hard school of experience, but that never again will the young minister have such an opportunity to live with the great disciplines of seminary training, the Old and New Testaments, Church History, Theology and Christian Ethics. There is much more, of course, that the minister should know but at least he must have a solid grounding in his own special field. He cannot apply the gospel to the modern world unless he knows what the gospel is. I realize that for most theological students outside work is a financial necessity. But I am confident that this should be kept to a minimum. All the rest of his life, the average clergyman will be engaged in the practicalities of administration and of pastoral care. In the seminary by worship, by thought, by study he has the opportunity to build the solid and enduring foundation of his ministry. I write, let me remind you, after over thirty years in the most practical tasks of an active ministry. Perhaps I should feel more strongly my lack of certain techniques in this field or that. But far more I have felt the need of the fundamentals, and I am willing to admit, the old fashioned fundamentals, of theological education. The medical student spends four years in a medical school, then at least two and perhaps five years in an internship at a great hospital. With only three years of seminary training available, it is important that first things be kept first. This means as I have suggested, hard intellectual effort, but even more necessary is the deepening of the wells of the spirit. There is a great danger that we become too familiar with sacred things and forget that knowing about religion or discussing religion is no substitute for its practice. It is unhealthy to talk about prayer and not to pray, to debate the nature and teaching of the Master without trying to follow him. The act of faith is not in knowing about God but knowing Him in a deep personal relationship. The years in a seminary if rightly used are much more than an academic requirement. They may and should be years of increasing wisdom and stature of growing in the knowledge and love of God. So the student is ordained not in the conviction that he, because of his gifts and learning, can enter a profession but because humbly and earnestly he has responded to the call of God.

The clergyman's primary task, let me say again, is to testify to the reality of the living God. I do not underestimate for one moment the other important functions of the Church and of the minister, such as the administration of relief, the organization of parish life, the responsibilities of community leadership, or even the privilege of sheer friendliness. All of these have their place. But the distinctive quality of the Christian minister is that by virtue of his calling he stands for God. This, offhand, should seem to be taken for granted. But the temptations which confront a minister are many and extremely subtle. It is not difficult to be led astray by administration, community service, popularity or a desire for social recognition. These are largely the temptations which come to the so-called successful clergyman with a considerable congregation and an assured position. But there are also dangers confronting the minister who has served long in a small parish with no calls elsewhere or has found himself in many similar positions even when he has moved. He has the problem of a small salary, and never the exhilaration of numbers, of organization and of public response. He must face the temptation of losing his own drive and initiative and of having his spirit broken. He may continue his ministry because there is nothing else that he can do but he only goes through the necessary motions. The one answer I know to these problems which face us all, whether our parishes be large or small, is constantly to re-examine our lives, goals and habits in the light of our primary responsibility. The ministry can become complex and confusing and the minister equally so unless he has the courage to come to grips with himself in the presence of God and to re-center his life in Christ. What is success or failure in the eyes of God? "He that is greatest among you, shall be the servant of all." Nothing else is of eternal significance. To stand for God demands an essential humility. The clergyman is an interpreter of God to his people, therefore he must be careful not to stand in the way of God. To be able to say, "Thus saith the Lord" as did the prophets of old is a fearful responsibility. There is an essential givenness. This message is not a man's own, in one sense, devised by his own prejudice or interest. It is God's. Thus saith the Lord speaking through him. The laity are almost pathetically patient with our sermons for in almost every congregation there is generally someone who is better informed upon any possible topic than is the clergyman himself. The principle of many a sermon may be true to God and then a mistaken illustration may destroy the whole effect. Which reminds me of an injunction of Dean Hodges, "When you are in the country, take your illustrations from the city, and when in the city from the country, it is safer." But people remain patient and yet eager because they have faith that the preacher has been called by God to this ministry, that by study he has come to understand at least some measure of the teaching of the Master and especially that in his vocation he has lived in daily companionship with the Christ. There must be complete integrity in the sermon for it is dedicated to God. Despite all the discouraging factors in the modern world, men and women, beset with fightings within and fears without, consciously or unconsciously long for God, if haply they may find Him. That is why those who are in church are there. They look to the minister as a representative of God. Therefore this responsibility must be a constant part of the minister's life. The services of public worship must be conducted with minute care and reverence because God "is in his holy temple. Let all the earth keep silence before him." The sermons must carry the over- and undertone of God's judgment and His seeking love. Parish calling, of which I shall speak later, can only have meaning as a means of bringing God into the homes and the personal lives of people. Especially, of course, must the minister's life speak of God. He may and ought to be humble in himself and yet strong in the dignity and supreme significance of his calling. Low and cheap standards even when they appear to gain popularity are a tremendous mistake. A minister must so carry himself that first of all he has the respect that leads men and women to bring to him their deepest burdens, temptations and problems. They must feel that he is one who has been with Jesus. I have seen clergymen irreparably injure their ministry through evident selfishness. A man who is self-seeking for place or comfort or salary cannot be convincing when he attempts to preach the gospel of unselfish service. It may not be fair for lay people to have a double standard for the clergyman and themselves, but nevertheless it is an unconscious tribute to the inherent worth of his calling. The laity expect to see in him what they know in their hearts they should be. A minister must always bear in mind

*143*

the admonition of St. Paul, "If meat maketh my brother to offend, I will eat no flesh." In all that he does he must bear in mind the effect upon the weakest of the brethren. As he serves God who is no respecter of persons, he must care equally for all with whom he comes into contact and not merely those who are congenial or who can do something for him, his family or even his parish. There were chaplains in the war who were known as officers' chaplains because they spent their time with the officers and cared so little for the enlisted men. These chaplains ended by being respected by no one. A similar condition is not unknown in civilian life, and does the Church no good. It may be objected that I have drawn a hard portrait of the minister and described a man who is stern, self-righteous and humorless. Nothing could be further from the truth unless we believe that such characteristics are true of the Christian. In this connection I think so often of Phillips Brooks. Certainly no man ever had a higher ideal of the ministry—yet no man was more intensely human in the best use of that much abused word, informal, in opening his own door to callers, in making parish calls, getting down on the floor to play with the children of his parishioners; he was witty, warm-hearted in his personal relationships. His religion was as natural as breathing. It was that very quality which helped to make him what he was. I joined the staff of Trinity Church nineteen years after his death. I expected to hear of his preaching, but equally one heard of his humanity, of his bringing coal on his shoulder to a woman in need, of his calling once a week upon a helpless cripple—always bringing the cheer of faith and of hope. A minister can be the most human person in the entire community with the true radiance of the religion of Christ, and still remind people of those deep spiritual truths which he preaches. There are many pitfalls. There is the stuffed pomposity of the ecclesiastic who always stresses his privileges and rights and who thinks of himself much more highly than is justified. But there is the equally absurd mannerism of the hail-fellow-well-met type who is fearful that someone will think that he has a serious purpose. There are many ways in which we can and do fall short of the glory of God. The answer is to live consciously and unconsciously in the presence of God. This is the only cure both for over-importance and for a sense of inferiority. Forbes Robinson in one of his ordination addresses said, "You have not simply to come to men as an inspiration but if I may use the expression—as a revelation." [2] The best and the worst aspect of the minister is shown in what he is. This means the ut-

[2] *College and Ordination Addresses,* p. 155, Longmans.

most of sincerity. The ministry is not a career or a profession but a life. There can be no vacation from this responsibility. The minister must be the same at play or at work, out of the chancel or the pulpit as in conducting a service of public worship. As Forbes Robinson went on to say, of a minister's relationship to a man, "You must give him an opportunity of seeing Christ, not as a distant figure in history, not as an ideal character in a book, not as a founder of a great institution; but as a human, a divine person, living, moving, working in you. Live Christ before his eyes. Demonstrate to him that man can rise higher than he dreams of. Reveal to him the spiritual life and he will cease to doubt its existence. Let him see how a man can be changed who yields himself body and soul to Christ's power. What possibilities there are in this weak human nature when Christ comes into it and so possesses it that a man may say, 'I live yet not I but Christ that liveth in me'." [3]

It may well be said, "Who is sufficient for such a task?" The answer is concise, "No one of us." The wonderful result is that despite our failures God does use our ministry, for all things are possible to Him. The clergyman stands on no special pinnacle, exempt from the temptations which come to all. Indeed the nearer he is to Christ the more he will ask forgiveness

[3] *Ibid.*

for his weakness. That very fact will make him more understanding of his people and more compassionate in dealing with them and with their problems. For he stands in the same need of God's forgiveness as do they. The redeeming factor in the situation is that the minister stands not for himself in the pride of knowledge or of position or of character. His primary task is to stand for God.

The second great privilege of the clergyman is to serve his people—of every background, occupation, and gifts. If he is awake to his task, he comes into intimate contact with an entire cross section of his community. It always amuses me when some one suggests that a clergyman is so sheltered that he knows very little of life. Then I think of hospitals, county jails, state penitentiaries, juvenile courts, city tenements, slums, among both the rich and the poor, experiences of joy and of sorrow, of moral failure and great achievement. The real pastor sees more of real life than perhaps anyone else. The practice of constant parish calling is the basis of the clergyman's knowledge of his people. One of the peculiarities of parish work today is the failure to make parish calls. I hear this constantly from laymen who belong to small as well as large parishes. Many clergymen seem to feel that they can be compared to the physician or the psychiatrist who keeps office hours or who is called to the home in a special emergency. The difficulty with this point of view is that the very people who need religion the most are the least aware of the need, and are the last people in the world to call either at a parish house or a parsonage. Office hours have their place, but many of those who come enjoy a clerical audience and will be found to visit all of the clergy of a community. The minister who waits at home or in his office is missing a great missionary opportunity. I know full well all the difficulties of parish calling under present conditions, the apartment stairs, the distances in many places, the countless times that no one is at home. However, granted all of that, I know from experience that the effort would be worthwhile even if every one were out. For the next Sunday a surprisingly large proportion of those called upon will turn up in Church saying, "We must admit that we have slipped in regard to the Church. But we are glad that you have not forgotten us." The familiar saying is still true, "A house-going parson makes a Church-going people." A minister cannot know his people unless he sees them where they live. The difficulty with many sermons is that they hit no mark. An old lady once wrote me of her rector, "I get so tired of being scolded every Sunday for the sins of the British Empire in the treatment of Gandhi." I doubt if a man can preach realistically to his people, no matter how well educated and read he may be, unless he knows them as they are at home. This is not to suggest that sermons should be made up of personal stories of the week's parish visitations. We are all familiar with the disastrous results of such preaching. A woman once told me of a grievous temptation torturing her. She happened to be the wife of a clergyman and knew whereof she was speaking. As she reached the door to leave she turned and said, "Don't you dare to use me as an illustration for a sermon." The minister cannot be too careful of the trust placed in him by his parishioners as they tell him of their deepest problems. But parish visiting will point to definite human needs. Again and again by a conversation or a situation, a spark will be kindled which will lead to a sermon based not upon theory but upon the reality of daily living.

There are clergy who say that they have no time to call unless there is an emergency. We shall all agree that emergencies should come first. Then certainly there can be no valid excuse for failure to give constant pastoral care. But regular parish visiting prepares the way for effective ministry in the emergency. In the course of years a crisis comes to every family and individual. When that comes a beloved friend is wanted and not a stranger. The ministry is essentially personal. When death or illness or some valley of the shadow appears, only one known and trusted can be of help. The parish call prepares the way and furthermore afterwards brings healing and peace. For the test of character comes not simply when the strain is greatest but in the long after-period of readjustment. It is not enough to conduct a funeral service and then to forget some one trying to build a new life in the face of a great loss. It is not enough to be present at the critical point in an illness and then to neglect the trying weeks of convalescence. A true pastor shares all these experiences year in and year out with his people. As I look back upon my years as a pastor, I have forgotten many of the administrative plans we had, the committee meetings I attended, but as long as I live I shall treasure the memory of opportunities of serving people personally and of trying, however inadequately, to bring to them the message of the love of God in Christ. The comment is made, that parish calls are a waste of time because only casual gossip takes place. If this be true it is the minister's own fault. It is possible to direct the conversation into helpful and sometimes deep channels. There are so many questions in people's minds and on their hearts, that with even a little encouragement they are glad to discuss them. A minister does not go merely as a friendly visitor but as a representative of Christ's Church. Many years ago I had an associate who was not an interesting preacher, he never could organize anything effectively. Fortunately he was an assistant and those responsibilities did not devolve upon him. He spent his life going in and out of homes serving and unselfishly loving people of every walk of life. He knew them, their grandparents and their grandchildren. When he died a great church was thronged with those who came to thank God for what he had meant to them. Today after twenty-five years people stop me to talk of him. With little of what might be termed professional success, in some ways he was the most truly successful clergyman I have ever known. I am not urging that one should be a dull preacher or an ineffective administrator but I am saying that, without this simple and unaffected love of people because they are the children of God, all else profiteth nothing. The minister should be the living exponent of the philosophy of the second mile. It is making the call, rendering this service which was not required, which really counts.

Finally parish calling saves the minister's own soul. It is possible to sit in a study and to lose all sense of proportion. Too many clergymen and their wives think that the minister works too hard and is not sufficiently appreciated. Too much time is spent in self pity and theoretical analysis. What a corrective it is to move out into other people's lives and to find those bearing infinitely heavier burdens with high faith and courage. The minister finds that he has received infinitely more than he has given. He inevitably forgets his own little problems, and his own soul is cleansed by losing himself in others. He may be depressed, then let him start a round of calls and he will come home thanking God that he is privileged to be a minister of Christ.

It is not easy to make regular parish calls. When the afternoon comes, there are so many other things which seem at the moment to be more important. It is necessary to make a definite plan and then to hold to this resolutely. I believe such a program to be essential.

It may seem that I have over-simplified the work of the minister in placing emphasis upon only two aspects of his work. But I believe that the heart of the ministry rests upon a minister's relationship to God in the sincerity of his own life and upon his moving in and out constantly and sacrificially among his people. With these two characteristics, many other things will be added unto him. Without them he may draw crowds, he may win awards for the best sermon of the current year, he may erect buildings and raise large budgets, he may receive ecclesiastical preferment but his ministry will be shallow and his success will be merely on the surface.

These characteristics of the love of God and of his people will be the basis of all he does. Let us take preaching as an example. The minister's desire should not be to make a great oratorical pronouncement which will enhance his own reputation as a public speaker but to be deeply helpful to his flock. There are few great preachers or great sermons. But there is no reason that there cannot be countless helpful preachers and sermons. When we try to be some one other than ourselves, we fail. A former teacher of mine said that he had seen a great many Phillips Brooks-lets in his day. Similarly today one can hear many preachers who have modeled themselves on some outstanding preacher. The voice, the delivery, the style are obviously if imperfectly there. But it is all second-hand and unnatural. Whatever else a preacher may be, he must first of all be himself. The failure to be this results simply in unreality and bombast. Bishop William Lawrence wrote, "Why, oh why, should a man who is cheerful all the week, who speaks to us pleasantly at ten o'clock in the morning as we meet him, strike a note of affected solemnity or anguish or perhaps shout as if noise were going to convert his hearers? Turn on the radio to several radio stations just before twelve o'clock on a Sunday, or even worse at half-past eight on a Sunday evening, and before you have heard a whole sentence you will know that a preacher and not a pleasant talker is on the air. One answer is this: when a man enters a pulpit he unconsciously enters into a pulpit tradition. Stand a layman in a pulpit and nine times out of ten he will have caught a preacher's tone and manner. I sometimes feel as if I would like to do away with every pulpit in the land and let the preachers begin again and, without the sermonic tradition, talk on religion as they talk in the homes of their people. Lay men and women have no conception of the training and self-control that every young clergyman has, or ought to have, to escape affectation or conventionalities and remain simple and real in chancel and pulpit. And every clergyman who does his duty is from ordination to his death alert to continue natural and be his best self." [4] In general we are too much given to broad exhortations on the state of the Church, the world and the Christian life, and too little attention is given to positive teaching. Our people are eager to know how to pray, what is the meaning of the Bible, how to meet the problems of daily living. They need simple directions as to the way of the Christian. Let a minister think of the requirements of his people as he knows them as a result of intimate personal knowl-

[4] In *The Church Militant,* "The Voice," April, 1938.

edge. Out of his background, training, reading and spiritual experience, he must have answers to their spoken and unexpressed needs. Then simply, naturally, sincerely and clearly let him state his position as the representative of God. Such preaching will be helpful and, because so, interesting. There can be no excuse for poorly-planned, discursive, dull sermons in the light of the character of the gospel and the great need of men.

Similarly in all he does the minister will be thinking of God and his people. One of the greatest problems a clergyman has to face is the use of his time, for no one can meet all the demands of preaching, of pastoral care, of the wider ministry beyond the parish and in the community. Whatever one does, it seems as if he should be somewhere else. It is wise to try to develop a plan, yet it must be remembered that a plan is made for man, and not *vice versa*. When there is human need the clergyman must be ready no matter what the inconvenience or the disarrangement. The practice of not being listed in the telephone book or of living as far from the church as possible has always seemed to me absurd. The clergyman must be at the center of life where the burdens are heaviest and where he may be reached easily by even the humblest of his flock. The only answer I know is the simple word "Work." Most of the people in the world are forced to work week in and week out. The minister is fortunate in that he is to a large extent master of his time. But therein lies a real danger that he easily deceives himself as to the amount of actual work he does. Let him think of many of his people in shop and factory. Given the utmost of his effort with the help of God he can so manage his life that the needs of his people will be met. After all he is a follower of One who gave his Life on the Cross. The ministry is hard and exacting to a degree but I would leave a false impression if I stopped there. The deep and abiding joy of standing for God, and of dealing with people in the deepest aspect of their lives, remains. I can honestly say that there is no life of more truly happy and abiding satisfaction.

It may seem that I have painted the picture of our contemporary world and Church somewhat out of focus. We have discussed some of the conditions of society and the Church, and then the resources of the spirit which are always available. Finally we have come to the work of the parish minister which may seem an anti-climax. But I doubt if this be valid. The Church rises and falls not alone by the plans drawn by great conferences, by the passage of resolutions, no matter how germane, but by the quality of life of the Christian. The parish minister is on the firing line. The parochial level is the important one for here are gathered the stuff of which the Church is made, men, women, boys and girls. What they are determines to a large extent the character of the Christian Church. All the machinery of the Church should bear upon this area. We have Church officials, theological seminaries, organizations, missionary effort at home and abroad in order that men and women everywhere should experience the knowledge and the love of God, and that, bound together in a living fellowship, they may show forth the fruits of the Spirit. One answer to the tragedy of our day is to be found in the lives of thousands of devoted ministers who in every nation, in city and rural areas, are humbly serving as reconcilers between God and men, and a man and his brother.

We have tried to face realistically the nature of our times. There is much to cause concern and bewilderment. No one can predict the future or see the solution to the problems confronting the nations. We have looked at the Churches and have found no cause for self-righteous complacency. The state of society today is not so much the judgment God has made upon us, as that we have brought upon ourselves by our failure to live in the light God has given to us beyond our deserts. The Christian can never become disillusioned or helpless. His faith rests not upon the shifting forces of contemporary society, not upon the success or failure of his own particular plans. His faith rests upon the will and the purpose of the eternal God. As we have seen, God reveals Himself in many ways, in the natural world, in the events of history, in the lives of men and women, even in spite of our unworthiness in the secret recesses of our own minds and hearts. Supremely God has revealed Himself in Jesus Christ, in the simple fact that he came, in the wisdom of his words, in all that he was, in his death and resurrection. When men are bewildered and the way ahead seems dark and uncertain, his light shines the brighter. When I was a chaplain in the first world war I carried constantly a cross. Many a time a dying soldier, too weak to speak or to hear a prayer, would take that cross in his hand and thus find behind that symbol the source of courage and of hope. So it is with us. The suffering and the sorrow of our day cannot be met by any shallow philosophy but only by the Cross of Christ which is the supreme testimony to God's redeeming love. There can be no hope for men except in the faith of eternal life—the gift of God. The world is either a meaningless tragedy or it is God's world. There is the choice which confronts every man and every generation, and which presses so desperately upon us all today.

In such a time we can be grateful that we either are, or are about to become, ministers of the gospel of Jesus Christ. There can be no calling more significant and none of greater privilege. For again let me repeat that the primary problem is spiritual. The minister strikes directly to the very heart of the world's need as he proclaims the eternal message of God. It is a task which is worthy of all we have, of all we are.

# INDEX